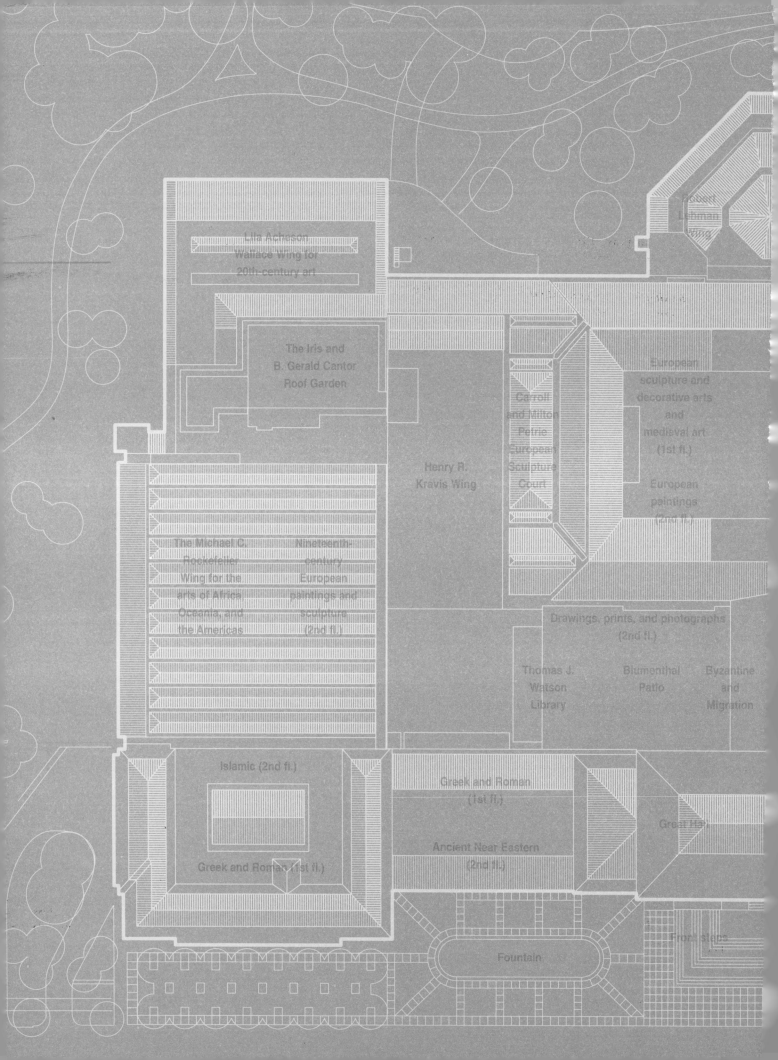

THE MET AND THE NEW MILLENNIUM

A Chronicle of the Past
and
A Blueprint for the Future

PHILIPPE DE MONTEBELLO

DIRECTOR

THE METROPOLITAN MUSEUM OF ART

Front cover: Aerial view of The Metropolitan Museum
of Art, 1991
Inside covers and title page: Plan of the Metropolitan
adapted from a drawing by Kevin Roche John Dinkeloo
and Associates

Reprinted from The Metropolitan Museum of Art
Bulletin (Summer 1994) © 1994 The Metropolitan
Museum of Art.
Design: LaPlaca Design Inc.

Director's Note

This issue of the *Bulletin* provides an account of the Metropolitan Museum's Master Plan, launched in 1970. I discuss how it evolved, how the Plan has changed as we have moved forward, and what are some of our initiatives for the future.

In reviewing this extraordinarily ambitious undertaking—an undertaking so large that its only recent equivalent in the museum world is the Grand Louvre—I also examine the reasons that led us to have made these changes and those that inform our future projects. These reasons constitute our philosophy, and they explain the very essence of an art museum. Although much of this philosophy is expressed, naturally, at the beginning and at the end of this narrative, it is also interwoven throughout the text so that accounts of the building program are presented not merely in an archival manner but with commentary and evaluation to place them in the context of our purpose.

If we have been able to achieve so much in the last quarter century and if our future continues to appear so promising, it is due to the many friends of the Museum whose generous pledges provide support for so much that we do. A number of these donors are acknowledged in this *Bulletin*, and while space constraints have not allowed for all to be mentioned, our gratitude to them is no less genuine and profound.

To one and all I express my deepest appreciation for their—and for your—understanding of and devotion to our fundamental mission.

Philippe de Montebello
Director

The 1970 Master Plan:

A Quarter Century of Growth

There are moments in the life of an institution—whether prompted by a celebration such as the Metropolitan's centennial in 1970, by an awareness that we are at an important crossroads, or, quite simply, by a sense that the time seems right—when it is useful to ponder past, present, and future. Certainly, the magnitude of our physical expansion in the last quarter century, of our dramatically increased attendance, and of the scope of our international collaborations—from scholarly exchanges to exhibitions—attests to a degree of maturity and to a new vitality at the Metropolitan that merit commentary and reflection. We should consider, for example, the implications of the rise in attendance from an average of 3 million visitors a year in the 1960s to more than 4.7 million today and review the wide spectrum of services that we provide for our public.

Now that we have completed the major part of the 1970 Master Plan—literally doubling the size of the Museum—it seems an especially appropriate time to reflect on this truly remarkable accomplishment, as henceforth we will be able to expand only within the existing footprint. This is a good moment, too, on the eve of our 125th anniversary in 1995, for us to redefine some of our goals and outline some of our plans for the future.

Because so much of this publication deals with the physical growth of the Museum, an unprecedented addition of about 1 million square feet of space (approximately 100,000 square meters), it is also pertinent to answer here, once again, the question often asked when the Master Plan was being developed: "Why expand—isn't the Met already too big?" The answer to this question remains timely and important: timely because the reasons for the physical expansion should continue to be properly understood; and

Opposite: The Great Hall, completed 1902. Refurbished in 1970 with funds provided by Lila Acheson Wallace

Above: The Museum at the morning opening, Christmas week, 1993

*Left: On the Great Hall balcony, **Perseus with the Head of Medusa**, by Antonio Canova, Italian. Marble, 1804–1806. Fletcher Fund, 1967*

In the 20th-century, Roman, and Egyptian galleries

Right: **Autumn Rhythm (Number 30)**, by Jackson Pollock, American. Oil on canvas, 1950. George A. Hearn Fund, 1957

Below: Roman sarcophagus, early 3rd century A.D. Rogers Fund, 1947

Opposite: Fragment of doorjamb from Temple of Ramesses II. Thebes, Dynasty 19, ca. 1304–1237 B.C. Gift of Edward S. Harkness, 1913

important because the answer tells us much about the nature of an art museum and particularly about that of The Metropolitan Museum of Art.

Simply put, the Metropolitan Museum could already have been considered "too big" in 1926, the year the McKim, Mead and White structure, including the Fifth Avenue façade, was completed. Put another way, any museum that is larger than, say, the Frick Collection, in New York, can be characterized as "too big," because it cannot be "done" in a day. Visiting the entire Metropolitan in the way one winds around the galleries of the Frick, or around our own Cloisters, would represent little more than taking inventory of what is on view. But the point of the Met is that it is not meant to be "done" in a day, any more than one should try to listen to all nine Beethoven symphonies in an evening or to read all of a library's books in a single sitting.

The Metropolitan is a collection of museums, each deserving of many repeated visits. It is a vast storehouse of knowledge, where works of art are held for reference and study as well as for display; its collections are meant

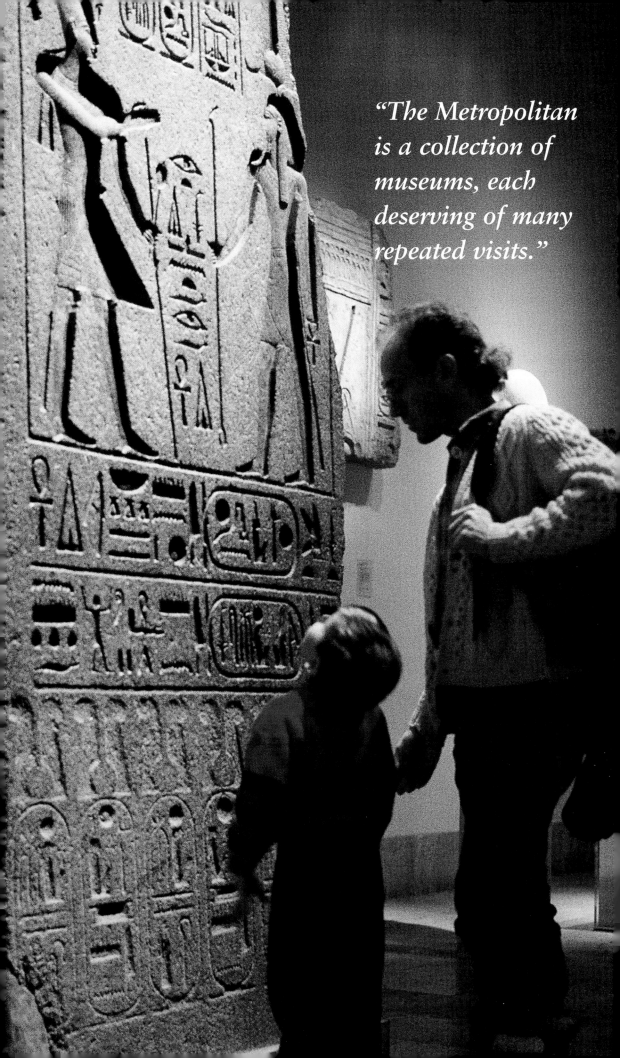

"The Metropolitan is a collection of museums, each deserving of many repeated visits."

CARROLL AND
MILTON PETRIE
EUROPEAN
SCULPTURE
COURT

In the Carroll and
Milton Petrie European
Sculpture Court,
opened 1990, Ugolino
and His Sons, by Jean
Baptiste Carpeaux,
French. Marble,
1865–67. Purchase,
Fletcher Fund,
Josephine Bay Paul and
C. Michael Paul
Foundation, Inc., and
Charles Ulrick and
Josephine Bay Founda-
tion, Inc. Gifts, 1967

to be consulted as one chooses from a long menu. Indeed, the strength of the Met is that all under one roof it provides an almost infinite number of options for many rich and rewarding visits. These can take an infinite number of forms, from random wanderings to planned itineraries, from an in-depth study of a single gallery or exhibition to the exploration of several different cultures or periods. Every conceivable peregrination is possible because the Met is a universal museum: every category of art in every known medium from every part of the world during every epoch of recorded time is represented here and thus available for contemplation or study—and not in isolation but in comparison with other times, other cultures, and other media. Understood in this way, of course, the Met can never be too big, for once we acknowledge that it can be visited best only in sections, in small tastings, then, as with a long menu or a box of assorted chocolates, the more we have to choose from, the better.

Above: Margaret Lawson, associate conservator, and William D. Wixom, Michel David-Weill Chairman of Medieval Art and The Cloisters, with the Beatus Manuscript. Spanish, late 12th century. Purchase, The Cloisters Collection, Rogers and Harris Brisbane Dick Funds, and Joseph Pulitzer Bequest, 1991

Left: Philippe de Montebello, director, in the Florence and Herbert Irving Galleries for the Arts of South and Southeast Asia before their opening, spring 1994

But here this analogy ends, for in addition to the dazzling variety of its public activities, there are many other, less visible dimensions to the Museum—far more than what may strike the eye of the casual visitor on any one day. For placing works of art on view is not simply a physical act; rather, it is the result of a long and intricate process of study and evaluation, of a multitude of crucial functions that are the particular province of the art museum and that allow for no short-cuts. For the most part, visitors are not aware, nor should they be, of this process.

Placing a work of art on view represents the culmination of a whole range of critical

curatorial tasks performed daily throughout the Museum and especially the quality of mind that informs our decisions about art. These are the decisions taken by a superb staff of highly trained specialists, curators, and conservators who complement one another's skills and knowledge. All are armed with years of intense study and looking, and their work is supported within the institution by well-stocked libraries and funds designated for travel and research, as well as by a host of specialized departments—all of which can be found listed in the Museum's *Annual Report*. Among those, one would find the Registrar, the Accessions and Catalogue Department, the Design and Editorial departments, the Photograph Studio, and many others.

Central to the process of presenting a work of art is the role of scholarship and connoisseurship. This is an important point, for we often list "research about the collec-tions" as among the highest priorities of the art museum, along with educational programs for the general public. Indeed, all that we do, we do with the overarching aim of reaching and enlightening the public, which, quite rightly, looks to us for truth. Yet truth is rarely an absolute when considering a work of art, for part of the

Opposite: Conservator Jack Soultanian Jr. with Jean-Antoine Houdon's marble Bather. French, 1782. Bequest of Benjamin Altman, 1913

Above: Malcolm Daniel, assistant curator, Maria Morris Hambourg, curator in charge, and Jeff L. Rosenheim, curatorial assistant, in the Department of Photographs

Left: Peter Antony, production manager, and Gwen Roginsky, chief production manager, compare color proofs in the Editorial Department

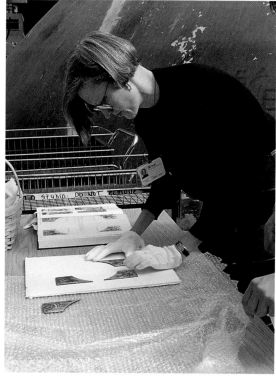

nature of a work of art is that it can never be fully known empirically.

Unlike almost any other "commodities" or "things," works of art are not always quite what they seem to be, especially in the case of those not made by our contemporaries. Judgments of quality aside—since these have no claims to total objectivity— we find that over time attributions, dating, and interpretation may change; even the assignment to a particular culture or country of origin may be revised. Also, we ourselves can change in our perceptions vis-à-vis a work of art. So the collections are—and must be—constantly under review. Matters of scholarship and connoisseurship being ever fluid, each succeeding generation may well and with full justification decide to reinterpret, reinstall, or reorder the collections. Indeed, it is not rare to find curators electing to retire to study-storage areas or to retrieve from them that which their predecessors valued differently.

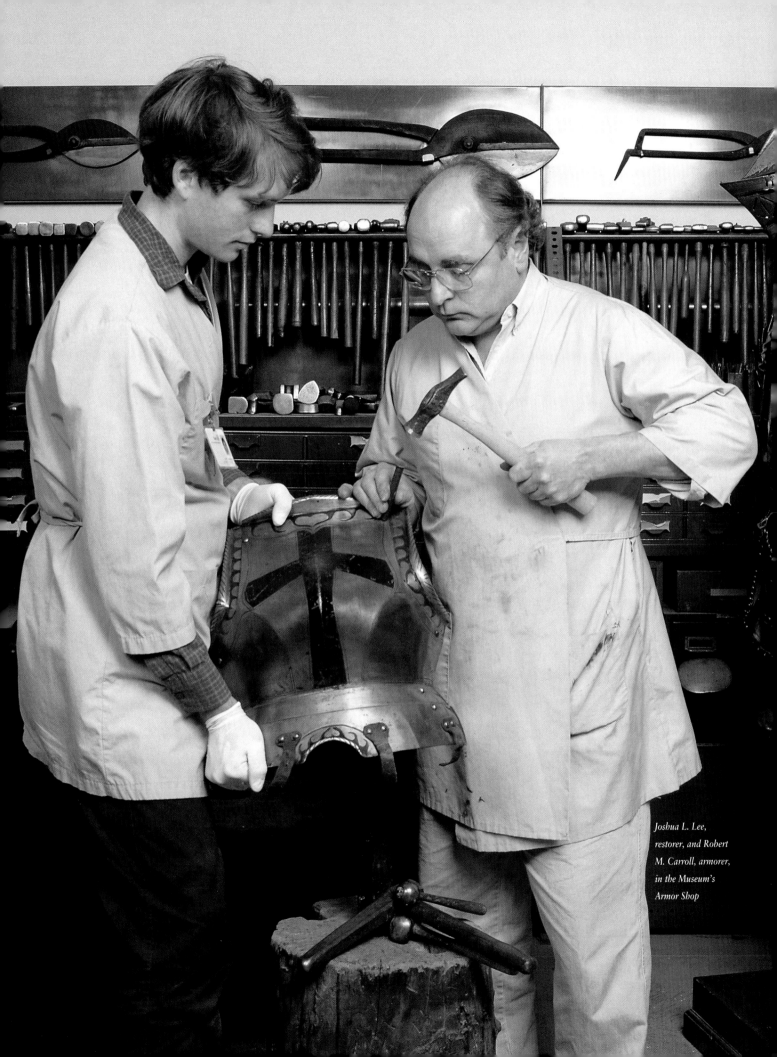

Joshua L. Lee,
restorer, and Robert
M. Carroll, armorer,
in the Museum's
Armor Shop

Therefore it is instructive to be aware of what lies behind the decision to put a specific work of art on view, where to place it, and what to write on the accompanying label. In fact, when confronted with a work of art, whether already in the collection or being considered for it through acquisition, curators must ask a host of questions, questions that they will never cease asking—nor will their successors—for works of art do not come with instructions or installation kits. The answers are what constitute our knowledge of the work of art, knowledge that the Museum has a duty to acquire and share; without it the Museum would be little more than a mindless assemblage of puzzling objects.

Sometimes even the most basic questions must be posed. "What is it?" might sound elementary, but occasionally the answer is not an easy one: iconography, style, or even weight might determine if the object, such as a piece of jewelry, was actually to be worn or to be a funeral ornament. It is important to know as much as possible about who made the work of art, where it was made, and why. What is its provenance? What is its condition?

This last is of far more than purely technical interest, for the answer tells us how close or how compromised and far removed the object is from its original state. And when some of these questions have been satisfactorily answered, we ask what may be the most important ones of all: How good is it? And how does it compare to the best in its category?

Only by asking questions like these can we ensure that what is displayed at the Museum is the result of diligent, careful, and informed selection and the exercise of rigorous scholarship and connoisseurship. If pleasure and instruction are then derived from a Museum visit, as we would wish, it is because the ordering and presentation of all aspects of the collections have been continually informed by the knowledge, intelligence, and sensitivity of a superb—indeed unsurpassed—staff of museum professionals. These remarkable men and women, no less than the collections, are what make the Metropolitan the great institution that it is.

The collections are the raison d'être of the Museum, and the primary stimulus for the 1970 Master Plan was their dramatic growth since the last major addition to the building in 1926. In fact the collections had so outgrown the spaces available that only an unacceptably small number of our finest works of art could be put on view. Thus there was an urgent need for new permanent galleries as well as for better public access.

Equally pressing, although less evident, was the need for improved and enlarged conservation facilities to reflect the tremendous technical advances made in this field and a new consciousness of its importance to the preservation and understanding of works of art. Moreover, a far more active exhibition program mandated the creation of new special-exhibition galleries—a goal we have now achieved—and larger and more efficient art-handling and receiving areas. While the latter have been improved somewhat, the level of the Metropolitan's loan activity has risen so dramatically in the last twenty years that more space for these critical functions still needs to be found.

Another imperative was the development of proper storage for the vast portions of our collections not on public view—those indispensable resources of any serious encyclopedic institution. Many of these works were housed in small, poorly climate-controlled areas, where they were not only at risk physically but also largely inaccessible to both the public and the staff. To cite an example, even now, at this writing in early 1994, the curator in charge of the Department of Islamic Art since 1988, Daniel

The Fifth Avenue plaza and front steps in 1985. Inset: Visitors crowd the narrow upper steps before the 1970 renovation and widening

Right: Elena Phipps (center), conservator, conducting a dry run of Antonio Ratti Textile Center shelving

Below: Maintainers David Mendez and T. C. Cusie cleaning the pool in The Charles Engelhard Court in The American Wing

Walker, an authority on oriental carpets, still has not been able to examine many of those in his department's collection, one of the world's richest, because they are stored in quarters so cramped that most cannot be unrolled. The Antonio Ratti Textile Center, scheduled to open in late 1995, will remedy this anachronistic situation.

It should be pointed out that the Textile Center (see p. 76) is but one of many major projects to address needs not met by the 1970 Master Plan. Although the Plan was a bold and far-reaching document, it could not possibly deal with every single requirement of the institution. Indeed,

if absolute comprehensiveness had been mandated at the start, we would still be quibbling about the relative importance of this collection or that department or fighting over details of space and square footage, and ground would not yet have been broken. Furthermore, as noted elsewhere but impossible to stress enough, the Metropolitan is a living organism; and as times change, so do priorities. The Met may be a giant, but it is neither lumbering nor unadaptive; on the contrary, it is remarkably flexible and willing to alter course when necessary.

Still another goal of the 1970 Master Plan was for better organization of interior facilities for day-to-day operations. The Metropolitan's building program from 1870 through the 1920s, rooted in the infancy of museology, had taken almost no account of what a modern museum must do behind the scenes to fulfill its mission, and little was done to remedy this deficiency between 1920 and 1970. Hence the space allocated to support functions up to 1970 was totally inadequate for modern requirements. How numerous and extensive these are can be seen in a quick glance at the back of any *Annual*

Report. Here, listed among the departments and staff members of this vast, complex organization are those responsible for the safety of the works of art—and of the visitor—and for the maintenance of the building; for the management of our $100-million-plus budget and our auxiliary activities, including shops and restaurants; for legal issues as well as for government and press relations; for membership and fund-raising activities, and so on. These services are all essential to the running of the Museum. Without addressing such critical areas—unglamorous, perhaps, but surprisingly interesting and varied in their functions—this museum's ability to serve the public in the 1980s, 1990s, and beyond would have been severely compromised.

Thus the Master Plan, developed with the Museum staff by the architectural firm of Kevin Roche John Dinkeloo and Associates, was launched in 1970, coincident with the centennial of the Metropolitan. Its purpose was to provide new space where necessary and to rationalize and upgrade existing spaces that had accrued in purely haphazard or opportunistic ways over the previous century.

Although the 1970 Master Plan was the first truly comprehensive plan formulated

by the Museum in almost half a century, thoughts of building and renovation had clearly occupied the minds of several directors before Thomas Hoving (1967–77). Indeed, it was under the directorship of Louis Palma di Cesnola in 1895 that the most ambitious but unrealized master plan in our history was elaborated by Richard Morris Hunt. More recently, in the summer of 1965, James Rorimer (1955–66), just a year before his death, devoted an issue of the *Bulletin* to the greater needs of the Museum. In an article entitled "Putting the House in Order," Rorimer offered some thoughts on a master plan, reminding readers that on several occasions previous administrations had toyed with the idea of actually demolishing the existing building and starting anew, so frustrated had they become with its

Above: Chris P. Giftos, coordinator, Great Hall and plaza, and manager for Special Events, changing the fresh flowers, a continuing gift of Lila Acheson Wallace

Left: Roy Walter, maintainer, in the Carpentry Shop

deficiencies in displaying the collections and serving the public.

Rorimer identified many of the problems later articulated in Hoving's master plan, but where the two directors differed was that Rorimer thought strictly in terms of the existing footprint and ameliorating spaces within, whereas Hoving broke out of the accepted mold, beyond the boundaries, to think in terms of true physical expansion. It was Rorimer, though, who recommended the changes to the front steps and plaza. His untimely death left this to his successor to carry forward in 1969, as a kind of preamble to the issuance of the Master Plan.

The renovations of the Fifth Avenue plaza, front steps, and Great Hall, completed in time for the 1970 centennial celebrations, were the first—and most dramatically visible—manifestation of the Museum's determination to adapt to a changing world,

one in which larger, more diverse, and more demanding audiences made it essential that visitor services be expanded and improved. Architecturally, it was natural to begin this task at the entrance to the Museum, at the point of first contact, where an unpleasant experience could mar an entire visit. Deemed crucial was the obligation to provide easier and safer access for the many thousands of daily visitors heretofore confronted with antiquated, uninviting, congested, and impractical entrances.

Until 1970 visitors entering the Museum were assaulted by a clutter of signs, sales desks, bulletin boards, and other paraphernalia encumbering Hunt's Great Hall, finished after his death by his son, Richard Howland Hunt, in 1902, and then and now surely one of the finest and grandest interior spaces in New York City. The year of its completion the Great Hall was described by a reporter as "a stately bride

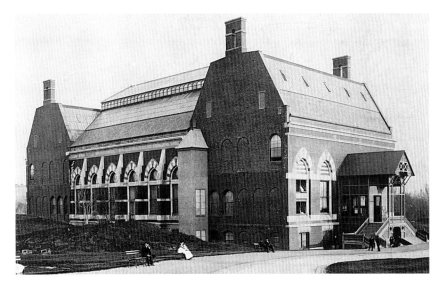

arrayed in spotless white"; but by 1970 the bride was an aging if still handsome matron, and anything but spotlessly white. So the hall was restored and refurbished with funds provided by Lila Acheson Wallace, founder with her husband, DeWitt, of *Reader's Digest*. She also established a perpetual endowment for the sumptuous fresh flowers that have delighted visitors ever since. Significantly, Mrs. Wallace funded the renovations not only of the Great Hall but also of the plaza and steps as the first of her many great benefactions, which together constitute the largest gift of funds (as distinguished from gifts of works of art) ever made to the Metropolitan Museum by a single donor.

Turning to the needs of the collections as recognized in 1970, we should note that the Master Plan was unquestionably triggered by a sense of urgency, with the approach of the American bicentennial, to enlarge the American Wing. The Museum's American art holdings had grown dramatically since the wing first opened in 1924, but the shell of the wing had never been increased; by the 1960s only 10 percent of the American art collections could be placed on view.

While the Master Plan discussions focused initially on the

American Wing, it was also observed that since the 1920s no additions had been made to areas of the existing main building, except isolated work such as filling in light wells or interior courts and the creation of the Grace Rainey Rogers Auditorium (1954) and the Thomas J. Watson Library (1965). So in the fall of 1967 Kevin Roche was retained as consulting architect, with expansion of the American Wing as his primary assignment. However, it soon became clear that the Metropolitan's growth by accretion, happenstance, and opportunity had produced a remarkably confusing floor plan—a patchwork quilt of disconnected spaces—and that the American Wing was only one of many deficient areas.

Thus Roche's initial assignment became part of a much broader and lengthier study.

The resulting Master Plan of 1970 was developed with full participation by the City and all of its appropriate agencies and groups. During this interval, August Heckscher, the administrator of Parks, Recreation, and Cultural Affairs of the City of New York, described the Met as "a drastically incomplete building, a hodgepodge of structures unsatisfactory both in external aspects and interior management and circulation." In fact, it was the Department of Parks that funded the development of the Master Plan, and it was the Parks administrator who signed the official publication of the comprehensive architectural plan for The Metropolitan Museum of Art, entitled *The Second Century,*

which was issued in January 1971. The City provided major support for Master Plan projects, including the American Wing, the Temple of Dendur in the Sackler Wing, the Lila Acheson Wallace Wing, the Henry R. Kravis Wing, and for the completion of a number of infrastructure needs.

In the years between 1967, when Roche was hired, and 1971, when the Master Plan was officially published, a number of important factors and events relating to the collections converged and became decisive in shaping other elements of the Master Plan. The four most significant of these were the need to enlarge the American Wing, which the City would approve only in the context of a master plan; the arrival of the Temple of Dendur, as a gift from the people of Egypt to the people of the United States, awarded in 1967 to the Metropolitan; the 1969 gift of the Michael C. Rockefeller Memorial Collection; and, in 1970, the gift of the Robert Lehman Collection.

The receipt of such vast collections and a whole Egyptian temple, nearly all at once and without funds to install them—nor, for that matter, even fractionally enough space in the building to accommodate them—would have thrown most administrations into a state of confusion. A less intrepid team than Board President C. Douglas Dillon and Director Thomas Hoving might have temporized,

Metropolitan Museum truly prosper only when they are at their most dynamic and confident. By the fall of 1971, thanks largely to his exceptional personal effort and leadership, major gifts were in place, starting with his own and including, among others, handsome donations from his fellow trustees Joan Whitney Payson, Arthur Houghton, Walter H. Annenberg, Jane Engelhard, Brooke Russell Astor, and Charles and Jayne Wrightsman.

Aerial views of the Museum taken in 1991 and 1955

In laying the groundwork for an enlarged display of the collections, those developing the Master Plan concluded that the ideal installation concept—unrealizable as it later turned out to be in most cases because of insufficient space—would be to give each

postponed difficult decisions, warehoused the collections, and launched a formal building-fund drive after ordering exhaustive studies. However, that was not Dillon's style as president. He believed institutions such as the

*Right: Students
at the information
light tables in the
Egyptian galleries*

*Below: The Charles
Engelhard Court in
the new American
Wing, opened 1980*

department its own primary galleries for the finest works, with complementary ancillary spaces for open-study storage, changing exhibitions, and general orientation. Only in the case of the Egyptian department has this notion been realized. Even there, however, the changing-exhibitions gallery opened only in 1993, thanks to a gift from the Malcolm Hewitt Wiener Foundation, Inc. Orientation in the Egyptian galleries, rather than taking place in a single space or room, as anticipated, was spread out, with light tables of didactic materials running the length of several galleries.

Other variations exist, as in the American Wing, which has no orientation area per se, but where the Henry R. Luce Center for the Study of American Art serves as the study gallery and the Erving and Joyce Wolf Gallery for changing exhibitions. Here, however, the Charles Engelhard Court meets another priori-

ty by furnishing a large area not only for the display of sculpture and for relaxation but also to create an indoor/outdoor feeling, visually reinforcing the relationship of the Museum structure and Central Park. This indoor courtyard idea, carried out first in the Engelhard Court and later in the Carroll and Milton Petrie European Sculpture Court, also serves to encourage the visitor to pause and take time to contemplate and assimilate what has been seen before moving on through the Museum.

I should stress here that the two functional objectives most consistently articulated in the 1970 Master Plan were to improve and enlarge the gallery spaces for the permanent collections and to enhance the nature and quality of the experience for the Museum visitor. Conservation,

24

art storage, administrative needs, and other support services were a distant third objective, with the result that many of those areas still very much need attention now, twenty-five years later.

To serve both coherence in the presentation of the collections and for visitor convenience an attempt was made to create broad geographic zones, grouping related curatorial departments within the building. Even with such a plan, however, there are very good reasons why we continue to adopt alternate methods of display. For example, not all of the European paintings are presented in the paintings galleries: two remarkable collections—the Robert Lehman Collection and the Jack and Belle Linsky Collection—are housed in their own galleries, which show the paintings with furniture, sculpture, and decorative arts.

The creation of period settings to display various kinds of art together has long been an important part of the Metropolitan, beginning with the American Wing in 1924. Starting in

In the Carroll and Milton Petrie European Sculpture Court, Sappho, *by Comte Prosper D'Epinay, Mauritian. Rome, ca. 1895*

proved woefully inadequate for their proper installation. It therefore became necessary by the late 1980s to assign to them the 10,000-square-foot gallery overlooking the Temple of Dendur in the Sackler Wing that is now devoted to Japanese art; the area had been used for special exhibitions, such as "Treasures of Tutankhamun," and earlier had been intended for various administrative and curatorial offices. To accommodate the much-augmented collections of Chinese and South and Southeast Asian art, other special-exhibition spaces, namely, those that had been used for the Vatican show, had to be relocated and assigned to the Department of Asian Art.

Above: The reading room in the Arts of Japan Galleries, built on the balcony overlooking The Temple of Dendur in The Sackler Wing, retains a window onto the temple and Central Park.

Right: T'ang-dynasty horse on the Great Hall balcony. Late 7th–1st half of the 8th century. Gift of Stanley Herzman, in memory of Adele Herzman, 1991

the 1960s, French furniture, decorative arts, and paintings were beautifully installed in a sequence of grand rooms donated by Charles and Jayne Wrightsman, the most recent of which was opened only a few years ago.

Although some of our visitors might prefer to see all of the European paintings in one set of galleries, others enjoy viewing them combined with furniture and decorative arts from the same period or kept together to reflect the taste of the original collector. At the Metropolitan you can view great paintings in many ways, which surely enriches the experience of the visit.

Meanwhile, during the 1970s and 1980s, our holdings of Asian art grew so far beyond our most optimistic expectations that the spaces we had allocated to them in the 1970 Master Plan at the north end of the building

Of the wings built since 1970 only the Lila Acheson Wallace Wing, located at the southwest corner of the Museum in an area originally allotted to European sculpture and decorative arts and then briefly to a media center, was not part of the Master Plan. At the time of the Master Plan, twentieth-century art was expected to be integrated into the American and European galleries, largely because the Museum was then more conscious of the inadequacy of its twentieth-century holdings than of their potential for growth. Indeed, in 1970, the Met's collection was characterized by Thomas B. Hess, writing as editor of *Art News* before his curatorial appointment at the Metropolitan, as "a collection of gaps." Thereafter, the Wallace Wing came into being partly because of the impassioned urgings, first of Henry Geldzahler, curator of twentieth-century art during most of the 1970s, and then of his successor, Tom Hess,

whose tragically short tenure was limited to the year 1978.

When Geldzahler became commissioner of Cultural Affairs under Mayor Koch, he helped persuade the City to share financial responsibility for the construction with the Lila Acheson Wallace Fund, headed by Mrs. Wallace's advisor Barnabas McHenry, to make the wing a reality. Also at this time, some of the most compelling voices for creating a

Above: Mezzanine sculpture gallery in the Lila Acheson Wallace Wing for twentieth-century art, opened 1987. This gallery is now designated the Blanche and A. L. Levine Court.

Left: Daylit room on the second floor of the Lila Acheson Wallace Wing

separate wing were those of potential donors of works of art clamoring for space. It was left to Tom Hess's successor, William S. Lieberman, Jacques and Natasha Gelman Chairman of the Department of Twentieth-Century Art, to shape the wing with its architect, Kevin Roche. The decision to create this wing has proven wise, as confirmed by a steady stream of major gifts, each of which has dramatically augmented and improved our collections of twentieth-century art.

Among the promised gifts, gifts, and bequests received were entire collections, such as that of Muriel Kallis Steinberg Newman, comprising sixty-four works that considerably strengthened our holdings of the American Abstract Expressionists. Two outstanding paintings in this group are de Kooning's *Attic,* of 1949, and Pollock's *Number 28, 1950.* The Scofield Thayer bequest in 1982 brought us Matisse's *Nasturtiums with Dance,* of 1912, which is perhaps the most important of the 342 works donated to the department, a group that is strong in art from the 1910s and 1920s, when Thayer, publisher of *The Dial,* was actively collecting.

Included in the gifts to the Department of Twentieth-Century Art in the last few years were several devoted to individual artists, creating splendid constellations of works by a number of major figures of this century. Among these are the ninety Paul Klees from the Heinz Berggruen Collection and ten Clyfford Stills given by his widow. The department has also made important purchases, such as Balthus's *The Mountain,* of 1937; and—adding to our

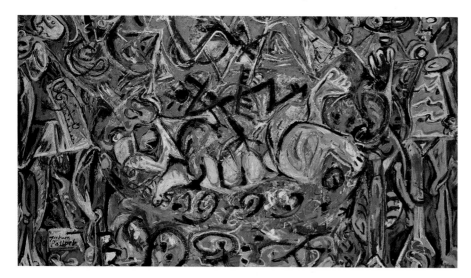

great strength in the works of Pollock—his masterpiece of 1943, *Pasiphaë*; as well as Lucian Freud's arresting *Naked Man, Back View*, of 1991–92, acquired with Lila Acheson Wallace funds.

It is axiomatic, of course, that collecting in an encyclopedic museum can never stop arbitrarily in time, and in this sense the decision in 1978 to devote a wing to post-1900 art in fact fulfilled the mandate of the founders. Their 1870 report called for a museum "based on the idea of a more or less complete collection of objects illustrative of the history of art, from the earliest beginnings to the present." We have always felt it right to construe "present" as a sliding frame of time; indeed, had we done otherwise and stopped collecting art created after 1870, most of our Impressionists and all of our Post-Impressionists as well, of course, as our twentieth-century collections would not have been acquired.

The first new wing of the approved Master Plan to be built was the so-called Lehman Pavilion, which was designed to house one of the most impressive private collections in the world. This collection, assembled by Robert Lehman, former trustee and chairman of the Board, and by his father, Philip, was presented to the Museum in 1970, just after the Master Plan study got under way. In scale it was a gift comparable to those of the Morgan and Havemeyer families.

The Lehman Collection is extremely strong in many important areas of European art. It numbers about 300 paintings, including a large group of very fine Italian panels of the fourteenth and fifteenth centuries and masterpieces of other schools, such as Ingres's *Princesse de Broglie* and Goya's *Countess of Altamira and Her Daughter*. There are more than 700 drawings, a group especially rich in the Venetian

school—thus adding strength to strength, as the Drawings and Prints department is also very rich in Venetian works. Among the stars of the Lehman medieval and Renaissance bronzes is a remarkable series of northern aquamaniles (containers for water), and the collection of decorative arts is particularly strong in Venetian glass and Renaissance majolica.

Because one of the conditions of the Lehman gift was that the works remain together, and since it was Robert Lehman's strong desire to retain the atmosphere of his house on West 54th Street in any reinstallation of the collection, several possibilities were explored. The first, to create a mini-museum in the existing 54th Street building, was ruled out, as it was just too small; the second, to re-create the house in the Museum's south parking lot, was also considered and rejected. The third and successful solution was a separate wing on the west side of the Museum, which would preserve the 1880 façade—a designated landmark—as its east wall.

Above: Seventeenth-century Dutch paintings in a Lehman Wing gallery

Center: **Phyllis and Aristotle**, *bronze aquamanile. Mosan school, ca. 1400. Robert Lehman Collection, 1975*

Left: **Punchinello as a Dressmaker**, *by Giovanni Domenico Tiepolo, Venetian. Drawing, late 18th century. Robert Lehman Collection, 1975*

The resulting Robert Lehman Wing, which opened in 1975, is a glass pyramidal structure with a central court and a surrounding two-story space, which has been the location for a number of major exhibitions, such as "The Horses of San Marco," "Painting in Renaissance Siena," "The Greek Miracle," and, most recently, "Petrus Christus." On the first floor are a series of galleries evocative of the principal rooms of the Lehman house. This year we were able to bring out of storage a glass dome designed for the house in 1904 and believed to be by Tiffany & Co. Once installed over the Lehman's main staircase, it now illuminates a small gallery devoted to jewelry, crystal, and glass.

The next priority of the Master Plan was to provide an enclosure to house the first-century B.C. Temple of Dendur, which had been dismantled into 642 stone blocks in Egypt, shipped to the United States, and stored since 1968 on the Museum's south parking lot in a plastic "bubble." The story of the temple and our success in winning it for New York demonstrate how willing the Metropolitan is to rise to a challenge, no matter how difficult the problem.

In 1965 the Arab Republic of Egypt offered the temple to the United States in recognition of U.S. financial aid in rescuing Nubian monuments doomed by the new Aswan Dam. Although several museums and cities, including Cairo, Illinois, were initially interested in receiving the temple, in the end our serious competition was Washington's Smithsonian Institution. While the Smithsonian maintained that the temple belonged outdoors, on the banks of the Potomac, the Metropolitan proposed an enclosed setting with a dramatic glass exterior wall, thereby protecting the fragile sandstone from the elements and pollution and at the same time providing natural light and a sense of the outdoors.

This scheme seemed to overcome earlier resistance to an interior installation, and when combined with the prospect of adjoin-

Above: Visitors in front of the Temple of Dendur

Below: The sandstone blocks of the temple, before reassembly, in a plastic "bubble" on the Museum's south parking lot, early 1970s

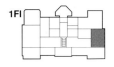

33

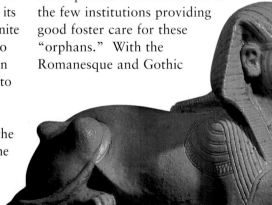

carved reliefs and, oddly enough for a Museum piece, graffiti cut into the walls by travelers from 10 B.C. and Early Christian times through the nineteenth century.

Among the French poet Paul Valéry's most acerbic—though not altogether unjustified—musings on museums is this: "There, painting and sculpture are orphans. Their mother is dead, their mother, who is architecture." Installations such as the Temple of Dendur suggest that the Metropolitan Museum is one of the few institutions providing good foster care for these "orphans." With the Romanesque and Gothic

The Temple of Dendur. Early Roman period, ca. 15 B.C. Given to the United States by Egypt in 1965, awarded to The Metropolitan Museum of Art in 1967, and installed in The Sackler Wing in 1978

ing the finest collection of Egyptian art in America, it assured that the Metropolitan would win the day. The chosen site, once the north parking lot, was transformed into a favorite destination for our visitors, who can view the temple from across a simulated River Nile and then take time to rest or dream in its presence, seated on benches around its granite tribune forecourt. The temple area has also served the Museum well as a grand location for social events from exhibition openings to corporate evenings.

This year, for the first time, we have permitted entry into the first chamber of the temple itself, where visitors can study the fine

arcades at the Cloisters, the Tiffany loggia and the United States Branch Bank façade in the American Wing's Engelhard Court, the Vélez Blanco Patio from Renaissance Spain, the sixteenth-century Indian Jain temple ceiling in the Florence and Herbert Irving Galleries, and the many period rooms—whether from Pompeii or Damascus, Bordeaux or Philadelphia—the Metropolitan does furnish an exceptional architectural context for many of its works of art.

The construction of the Temple of Dendur enclosure was part of a larger building program that included the north garage on the ground floor and related spaces. Thanks to the generosity of Douglas Dillon; the City of New York; Arthur, Mortimer, and Raymond Sackler; and several other donors, the entire project was completed in 1978 with the opening of the temple in

the part of the area known as the Sackler Wing.

The temple's inauguration followed by two years the completion of the first phase of the comprehensive reorganization of all of the Egyptian galleries. Begun with the goal of putting our entire reserve collection on view for the first time, this prodigious task,

Opposite inset: Photograph of the temple, by Félix Teynard, French. Ca. 1853. Purchase, Lila Acheson Wallace Gift, 1976

Left: Visitors inside the temple

Opposite below: Faience sphinx of Amenhotep III. Dynasty 18, 1391– 1353 B.C. Purchase, Lila Acheson Wallace Gift, 1972

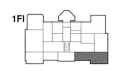

35

Clockwise:
Sculpture in the
Egyptian galleries.
In the foreground is
a limestone figure of
a bound prisoner.
Dynasty 5, ca. 2400
B.C. Louis V. Bell
Fund, 1964

Schoolchildren with
facsimiles of
Egyptian wall paint-
ings, principally from
Thebes, painted by
the Museum's
Graphic Expedition.
Rogers Fund,
1907–1939

Fragmentary head,
possibly of Queen
Tiye. Yellow jasper,
Dynasty 18, ca.
1391–1345 B.C.
Purchase, Edward S.
Harkness Gift, 1926

a reinstallation of about 70,000 square feet of space, was completed in 1983. Every one of the estimated 37,000 objects was put on display, including excavated material represent- ing thirty years of activity by the Metropol- itan's Egyptian Expedition from 1906 to 1936, which was placed in special open study areas adjoining the main galleries. We also installed in nearby galleries our collection of watercolor facsimiles of Egyptian wall paintings done by expedition artists, largely during the 1920s. These faithful copies of ancient wall paintings are becoming increasingly important because the surface of the originals has continued to deteriorate.

Concurrently with the massive Egyptian department reinstallation, we were planning the new American Wing, which, it will be remembered, had been a prime catalyst for the 1970 Master Plan. The wing was inaugurated in 1980 after an intensive period of construction and renovation requiring many highly specialized skills. Extensive conservation was carried out not only on architectural elements but also on furniture and other individual works of art.

The objective of the new wing was to combine under one roof our collections of American paintings, sculpture, and decorative arts. The old wing was to be encased in a larger building housing the first permanent galleries for American paintings and sculpture—the Joan Whitney Payson Galleries. The courtyard outside the old American Wing was roofed over and given a glass façade facing Central Park, creating the Charles Engelhard Court. On the ground floor, as noted, the court serves both as an indoor sunlit area for the visitor to enjoy and as an appropriate space for the display of nineteenth-century sculpture. But most important, as with the

The Charles Engelhard Court in the American Wing. Front: Saint-Gaudens's **Diana**. *Rogers Fund, 1928. Back: Tiffany's Laurelton Hall loggia. Gift of Jeannette Genius McKean and Hugh Ferguson McKean, in memory of Charles Hosmer Morse, 1978. Left: Vanderlyn's* **Panoramic View of Versailles**, *1818–19. Gift of Senate House Association, Kingston, N.Y., 1952*

Temple of Dendur enclosure, the Engelhard Court is an environmentally protective envelope for irreplaceable architectural works. The imposing 1822–24 façade of the Branch Bank of the United States from Wall Street, exposed to the elements in the old courtyard, is now enclosed as the court's north wall, and for the first time we are able to show the loggia designed by Louis Comfort Tiffany for his home in Oyster Bay, Long Island. The court also permits us to exhibit large works in stained glass and to incorporate the Louis Sullivan staircases from the 1893 Chicago Stock Exchange Building, fine examples of his highly personal ornamental style. We were able to install the stairs so that none of their functional character is lost: they provide public access to second-floor-balcony displays of silver, glass, and ceramics.

The old American Wing building, which was and still is devoted to period rooms, was entirely refurbished. A beautiful late Federal room from Richmond, Virginia, was added, and three mid-eighteenth-century rooms—Van Rensselaer Hall, Marmion, and Verplanck—were relocated

doors, to museums in Minneapolis, Allentown, Dallas, and Karlsruhe, Germany, thereby assuring that examples from this house are accessible to a broad public. The Frank Lloyd Wright Room, dating to 1912–14, establishes the temporal limits of the American Wing, although boundaries between the Department of Twentieth-Century Art and the American Wing naturally overlap.

Left: Looking out at Central Park from The Charles Engelhard Court. At left is Erastus Dow Palmer's The Indian Girl, *1853–56. Bequest of Hamilton Fish, 1894*

Below: **Fur Traders Descending the Missouri,** *by George Caleb Bingham. Oil on canvas, ca. 1845. Morris K. Jesup Fund, 1933*

next to galleries of decorative arts. Once the first phase opened and installation principles were established, work continued on the rest of the period rooms. Seven nineteenth- and early-twentieth-century rooms have been opened; the last, in 1991, is the stair hall from the 1884 Metcalfe House in Buffalo, New York, designed by McKim, Mead and White.

In 1971 the Metropolitan had learned of the impending demolition of Frank Lloyd Wright's Francis W. Little House in Wayzata, Minnesota. Realizing the need to save some remnants of this grand lakeside structure, we purchased the house and its contents, carefully dismantled the structure, and put everything in storage. As it was our intention to install only the living room, one of the largest Wright designed, we have sold over the years all of the other rooms, as well as many stained-glass windows and

As of 1994 all major areas within the American Wing are fully occupied, and there is no space for additional period rooms, only for individual objects and paintings acquired during the ongoing process of further "refining" the collection: that is, in museum jargon,

Right: The Melvin Memorial, by Daniel Chester French. Marble replica of 1908 monument to Civil War dead at Concord, Mass. Gift of James C. Melvin, 1912

Below: Silver in The Henry R. Luce Center for the Study of American Art, opened 1988

upgrading through judicious acquisitions and occasional deaccessioning. Conceivably, we could also upgrade among the period rooms if a spectacular example became available and if sufficient funds were found to permit a substitution. Considering the complexity of such a substitution, including finding a deserving home for the retired room, the decision would be a very difficult one. But the Metropolitan has never shunned the opportunity to make truly exceptional acquisitions; in fact, it owes its greatness in large part to a constant willingness to do so, and such a substitution, therefore, could possibly occur.

The Museum owns more than 15,000 American paintings, sculptures, and decorative arts objects, and until the 1988 construction of the Henry R. Luce Center for the Study of American Art, a good portion of this collection was kept in storage. The Luce Center, based on typology rather than qualitative arrangement, makes the more than 8,500 paintings, sculptures, pieces of furniture and decorative arts that constitute the study collection accessible to the scholar and the curious visitor alike. The visible storage concept grew out of the success of the Egyptian department's open study galleries, but the Luce Center went a step further with such features as an automated catalogue of the entire collection of the American Wing, with information on every object available at public computer terminals. Data are continuously revised and expanded to reflect ongoing research. The Luce Center also enables the department to stage small "dossier" exhibitions around aspects of the collections, such as "Portraits of American Artists in the Metropolitan Museum," held in 1992–93.

The American Wing is tremendously popular with the public, who ably navigate its mazelike floors on many different levels. Although the spatial complexity of the wing has defied the best mapmakers, its confusing signage and layout have clearly not deterred our visitors.

Only two years after inauguration of the new American Wing in 1980, we opened the Michael C. Rockefeller Wing on the south side of the building to house the very large collection of art from Africa, Oceania, and the Americas pledged by Nelson Rockefeller in 1969 and comprising in part objects Rockefeller had given to the Museum of Primitive Art, which he founded in association with René d'Harnoncourt in 1954. Including over 3,500 works and the unique resources of the Robert Goldwater Library, the Rockefeller gift was made in memory of his son Michael, who was lost on an expedition to New Guinea in 1961.

The Rockefeller Wing has a glass wall opening onto Central Park, similar to those of the Dendur and American wings, and this south gallery's great height permits the display of very large objects such as the towering Asmat *mbis*, or ancestor poles. The

Robert Goldwater Library, named for the first director of the Museum of Primitive Art, was constructed on the mezzanine and continues to serve as an invaluable research facility for the general public as well as for scholars.

The Metropolitan has been acquiring the arts of Africa, Oceania, and the Americas since the late nineteenth century, when a pair

Above: Art of Oceania gallery in The Michael C. Rockefeller Wing, opened 1982. At right are Asmat **mbis** *poles from New Guinea. Michael C. Rockefeller Memorial Collection, Gift of Nelson Rockefeller and Mrs. Mary C. Rockefeller, 1965*

Left: The Jan Mitchell Treasury for Precolumbian works of art in gold, opened 1993

of impressive eagle reliefs from Mexico was given by the American artist Frederic Church in 1893 and the Petich collection of Mexican antiquities was purchased in 1900. During the 1960s our Precolumbian holdings were strengthened by gifts of Peruvian ceramics from Nathan Cummings and by the first of the donations of ancient American goldwork from Alice K. Bache. In 1977 the Museum accepted from Lester Wunderman the first of several important gifts of West African Dogon art, constituting the initial display by the Museum of African art other than the Rockefeller gift.

Nearly fifteen years later Klaus and Dolly Perls gave a significant group of works from the African kingdom of Benin in Nigeria, and our Precolumbian goldwork was greatly augmented by the donation of major works from the Jan Mitchell and Sons Collection. Last year we opened the Jan Mitchell Treasury for Precolumbian works of art in gold, in which three major collections—those of Alice Bache, Nelson Rockefeller, and Jan Mitchell—were joined to form what is

the most comprehensive display of such gold objects in the United States. Also in 1993 we renovated the West African gallery, giving greater exposure to Dogon objects from the Wunderman gift. Currently, we are planning a redesign of the Central African gallery to include a sizable group of Benin works from the Perls gift, which made the Museum's collection of Benin art among the strongest in the world.

I think it is fair to say that only from the time of Nelson Rockefeller's 1969 gift could we legitimately claim that we were truly encyclopedic, truly a universal museum. Only with the opening of the Michael C. Rockefeller Wing could we further claim that at the Metropolitan the arts of Africa, Oceania, and the Americas were given their rightful place alongside those of other great civilizations of the world. The intermittent and itinerant displays of the few pieces we had acquired over the preceding century were well-intentioned first steps, but they could only hint at these regions' rich artistic traditions, traditions confirming that the thread of man's artistic creativity knows no boundaries of time or place.

Our Asian holdings had been formed, over nearly a century, through a combination of gifts and purchases, going back to the 1879 acquisition of the sizable Samuel P. Avery collection of Chinese and Japanese ceramics. For several decades thereafter the collections grew primarily in the area of decorative arts with gifts from well-known benefactors such as Edward C. Moore, Heber R. Bishop, the Havemeyers, Benjamin Altman, and John D. Rockefeller Jr. However, unlike other American museums such as Boston, Kansas City, or Cleveland—for whom acquiring Asian art was already a high priority—the Metropolitan was uncharacteristically lackadaisical in its collecting in this field, probably because of little support at the top. Fortunately, a few very strong areas—particularly our monumental Chinese Buddhist sculptures and ceramics—helped us maintain at least a modicum of reputation.

Thus by 1970, when we embarked on the Master Plan, it had been many years, even decades, since the purchases of our finest Chinese pieces. For example, our unique Chou-dynasty altar set had been bought in 1924; and in our small paintings collection the great Southern Sung work *Emperor Hsüan-tsung's Flight to Shu* had been here since 1941. Elsewhere, where our holdings were extensive, they were also uneven. The Benjamin Altman bequest of 1913, for instance, brought us first-rank eighteenth- and nineteenth-century ceramics, though not those of the more

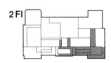

43

desirable early periods. And like the Altman collection, the Bishop jade collection was well known, but its strength also lay in late pieces rather than in the more desirable archaic period. Our holdings in Japanese art were even thinner, with, among their very few high spots, the much-reproduced Kōrin screen of irises (*Yatsuhashi*, or "Eight-plank Bridge") purchased in 1953. The Indian and Southeast Asian holdings were more anemic still. Korean art, unfortunately, remains a mere skeletal representation of a culture that will be owed its turn now that the other areas have been immeasurably strengthened.

However, in the past quarter century we have dramatically shifted our priorities to the collecting of Asian art, and as a result we have come to the point where we may now take pride in having built a collection that rivals the very best anywhere.

The impetus behind this change came from the Honorable Douglas Dillon, the Museum's president and chairman of the Board from 1970 to 1983, who urged Thomas Hoving to place greater empha-

Above: Summer Mountains, detail of handscroll attributed to Ch'ü Ting. Chinese, Northern Sung dynasty, 11th century. Gift of The Dillon Fund, 1973

Center: Red-lacquer dish. Chinese, Yüan to early Ming period, 14th century. Promised Gift of Florence and Herbert Irving, 1991

Right: The Astor Court, modeled on a Ming-dynasty scholar's retreat, opened 1981. Funds for the court and the Ming Hall at its north end were provided by The Vincent Astor Foundation.

sis on Asian art. Hoving appointed Wen Fong, professor of art history at Princeton University and noted authority on Chinese painting, to head the department. Hired in 1971, he restructured it, built a curatorial staff of international reputation, and with the help of Douglas Dillon, Brooke Astor, and other benefactors brought the Asian collections up to the eminent position they occupy today.

Dillon's enthusiastic support for the Museum's pursuit of the finest Chinese paintings and calligraphic works soon resulted in our collections of this material becoming some of the most notable in the field.

The opening of the Douglas Dillon Galleries and the Astor Court in June 1981 was the first public sign of the Museum's revitalized Asian art department. Response to Dillon's leadership from collectors of Chinese paintings and calligraphy has been extraordinary, with the most significant gift being that from John M. Crawford Jr., whose collection of over 100 superb paintings and calligraphic works propelled us, in one major stroke, to preeminence in this field. Other important gifts and promised gifts coming from, among others, Robert Hatfield Ellsworth and the P. Y. and Kinmay Tang family have caused us to consider an expansion of the Dillon Galleries—barely a dozen years after their opening—that will make them the largest permanent display space for Chinese painting and calligraphy in the Western world.

The Astor Court, a beautiful spot for contemplation adjoining the Douglas Dillon Galleries, is intended to provide a smooth and, as it turns out, also an idyllic transition from West to East. This garden court was the conception of Brooke Astor, a trustee from 1964 and first chair, now co-chair, of the Visiting Committee for Asian Art (formerly Far Eastern Art). Mrs. Astor spent part of her childhood in Peking and grew to love the enclosed courtyards in early Chinese buildings. The Museum's court, based on a Ming-dynasty example at Soochow, was assembled in traditional fashion in 1980 by craftsmen from that city. In fact, the Astor Court project, made possible through the generosity of the Vincent

Astor Foundation, was the first permanent cultural undertaking shared by the United States and the People's Republic of China.

The growth of our Japanese holdings has been inextricably linked to the interests of America's preeminent collector of Japanese art, Mary Griggs Burke, a trustee, member of the Acquisitions Committee, and co-chair of the Visiting Committee for Asian Art, who has contributed generously to purchases and provided invaluable leadership and impetus. Mrs. Burke, whose love of Japanese art grew out of her interest in modern art and garden design, made her first important purchase in 1956, an Edo-period screen painting of the *Tale of Genji*, which had once belonged to Frank Lloyd Wright. By 1966 she and her husband, Jackson Burke, had acquired

Left: The Astor Court was built almost entirely by Chinese craftsmen.

Below: Woman's robe (kosode). Japanese, Edo period, late 17th century. Tie-dyed and embroidered satin. Purchase, Mary Livingston Griggs and Mary Griggs Burke Foundation Gift, 1980

enough pieces to create a mini-museum of their own. By the late sixties and early seventies, Mary and Jackson Burke had developed a clear vision in building a representative collection of Japanese art spanning the entire development of that ancient civilization. It was evident that the Burkes' passion in bringing the best of Japanese art to a wider audience in this country was an inspiration to the Metropolitan, which was now determined to boost its Japanese holdings from inadequate to top rank.

During the early 1970s the Metropolitan was confronted with a unique opportunity to acquire a major private collection of Japanese art. Harry G. C. Packard, who learned Japanese at the U.S. Navy language school and stayed in that country after the end of the Occupation in 1950, put together a group of over 400 high-quality objects representing the whole history of Japanese culture, from the Neolithic period to the twentieth century. Recognizing the extraordinary nature of this opportunity, the Museum's entire curatorial staff, of all

the then seventeen departments, voted in an amazing display of near-unanimity to commit for five years a large portion of unrestricted acquisitions funds to the Packard purchase. For the Far Eastern department in 1975 this gesture was a critical affirmation of the growing importance of Asian art at the Metropolitan.

After completion of the Dillon Galleries and Astor Court, work began on the Arts of Japan Galleries to be installed in the Sackler Galleries for Asian Art, overlooking the Temple of Dendur. An important source of inspiration and support was again Mary Burke, who not only made grants through the Mary Livingston Griggs and Mary Griggs Burke Foundation but also was most helpful in our fund-raising efforts in Japan, which were led by Douglas Dillon. The result was a remarkable Japan-wide effort by companies and individuals—even schoolchildren— as well as by New York's Japanese community, to augment the Japanese government's

Galleries for South and Southeast Asian art), and highlights were published in a *Bulletin* in 1973. What is striking about that publication, written by Wen Fong and Curator Maxwell K. Hearn, is how many of the works illustrated—and, incidentally, not the least important ones—were loans, many of which, happily, have since been given to the Museum. In 1985 this tremendously significant area was further strengthened by the gift of a group of small, marvelous objects from the Ernest Erickson Foundation, including many fine Bronze-Age examples.

The Museum's commitment to this field has also been reinforced by Brooke Russell Astor Senior Curator James C. Y. Watt, working closely with collectors, principally with Charlotte C. and John C. Weber, whose generosity has been recognized by the appearance of their names on the galleries for the arts of ancient China as well as on credit lines of many major acquisitions of early Chinese art. It is also because of James Watt that a number of extremely fine and rare Chinese and Central Asian textiles were purchased. One of the last of these, and the grandest so far, is a Yüan-dynasty silk-tapestry mandala, the only surviving imperial commission from workshops within the Mongol empire (see p. 49).

In this context it is

(see p. 49).

initial gift, which was presented in 1979.

Elements for special gallery designs (derived from a temple and a *shoin* room) were made by Japanese craftsmen in Kyoto, and the galleries, blending the fine and decorative arts in a manner consistent with Japanese tradition, were set up for the frequent rotations that light-sensitive screens, doors, scrolls, textiles, and prints require. The historical presentation of Japanese art in a chronological sequence ends with a comfortable reading room for resting or watching video orientations and flower arranging. The link to contemporary Japanese culture in the galleries has been extended through a boldly abstract garden, *Water Stone*, executed by the sculptor Isamu Noguchi. This sliced basalt boulder, with water spilling over the top, is an evocation of the stone garden basin originally used for purification before entering a Shinto shrine or a Buddhist temple.

Early Chinese art, that from early Shang through the T'ang dynasty, was displayed for a number of years in the east galleries (the current Irving

Left: Buddhist altar platform modeled on a 12th-century example in Fuki-ji, Kyushu, in the Arts of Japan, The Sackler Galleries for Asian Art, opened 1987

Below: The Guardian King Fudo Myo-o. Japanese, late Heian period, 12th century. Wood, colors, and gold leaf. The Harry G. C. Packard Collection of Asian Art, Gift of Harry G. C. Packard, and Purchase, Fletcher, Rogers, Harris Brisbane Dick, and Louis V. Bell Funds, Joseph Pulitzer Bequest, and The Annenberg Fund, Inc. Gift, 1975

interesting to note how often some museum collections have their character conferred on them by the personalities of the individuals who formed them. Indeed, collectors can indulge their cravings, and even their obsessions, in a way that a public institution cannot. Mary and Jackson Burke, already mentioned in the area of Japanese art, are outstanding examples. Another couple indispensable to our Asian collecting odyssey is Florence and Herbert Irving, who first demonstrated their passion for Asian art with their purchases of lacquers—Chinese, Japanese, and Korean. Their lacquer collection, generously presented to the Metropolitan in 1991, is now the largest and finest in the West. On our own we might have acquired at most a few pieces, or barely a fraction of what the Irvings, unhampered by institutional constraint, could and did buy. The result is yet another field in which the Metropolitan can not only display fine representative examples of a single medium, style, or artist but also provide a critical body of objects to serve as a major resource for scholars. In the area of South and Southeast Asian art it was the mandate of Curator

Martin Lerner to bring the collection up to the highest standards. In a remarkably short time a great deal was accomplished, and we were strongly supported by a dedicated group of collectors and donors as well as by the substantial use of general Museum purchase funds. Among the major donors are members of the enormously generous Annenberg family, Enid A. Haupt, Lita Annenberg Hazen, Cynthia Hazen Polsky, and Walter Annenberg. To Ambassador Annenberg we owe the elegant tenth-century Cambodian Avalokiteshvara, which must be considered one of the finest bronzes to survive from the height of that civilization's artistic achievements.

The gift of more than 400 works from Samuel Eilenberg in 1987, combined with our purchase from Columbia University of twenty-four additional sculptures, transformed our holdings in two important areas, the early arts of India and Pakistan and the bronzes of Indonesia. The Kronos Collections have made many significant gifts since 1979, including a very rare pair of royal golden Indian earrings. These collections were formed for his family by Steven Kossak, associate curator in the Department of Asian Art and manager and coordinator for the installation of the new galleries for South and Southeast Asian art. Jeffrey B. Soref has also

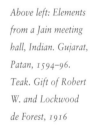

been generous in sharing with the Museum and the public through gifts and loans important early works, such as the Yaksha and Yakshi near the entrance to our new galleries, which enable us to represent the monumental sculptural tradition of India from the first century B.C. Finally, we have again found strong advocates for this field in Florence and Herbert Irving, who have donated a substantial group of objects as well as the funds required for building the galleries that now house our South and Southeast Asian collections and that bear their names.

The Florence and Herbert Irving Galleries, covering 15,000 square feet and running the length of two city blocks, constitute the largest space anywhere dedicated to the arts of South and Southeast Asia. Naturally, because of their colonial histories, one finds more Indian art in London, more Cambodian art in Paris, and more Indonesian art in Leyden; but in none of these cities does one find all the cultures of this region so broadly represented as they are here. In designing these

rooms to house so many different cultures from such a wide area of the globe, evolved along parallel courses over three millennia, we created spaces distinctive in their volumes and evocative in their materials, finishes, and architectural treatment of many of these regions.

The Irving Galleries can be entered through either the Douglas Dillon Galleries or the Arthur M. Sackler Gallery for Chinese sculpture, which has been handsomely renovated. A new ceiling with translucent glass now illuminates the recently cleaned Yüan-dynasty Buddhist fresco, and the monumental sculptures have been given more space around them. The massive limestone sixth-century pagoda sanctuary, acquired thanks to the Vincent Astor Foundation and Henry and Ruth Trubner, has been repositioned to reflect its original orientation, and the staircases leading to the Weber and Irving galleries have been widened to provide a grander access.

That such an extensive area is available for these Asian galleries is of course due to completion of other parts of the Master Plan, the Wallace and Kravis wings to the south, within which we have been able to provide two major spaces exclusively for special exhibitions, namely, the Iris and B. Gerald Cantor Exhibition Hall and the Tisch Galleries.

Above left: Elements from a Jain meeting hall, Indian. Gujarat, Patan, 1594–96. Teak. Gift of Robert W. and Lockwood de Forest, 1916

*Above right: **Standing Buddha**, Sri Lanka. Polonnaruva, 11th–12th century. Gilt bronze. Gift of Enid A. Haupt, 1993*

Left: Detail of a silk-tapestry mandala, Chinese. Yüan dynasty, ca. 1328. Purchase, Lila Acheson Wallace Gift, 1992

With the construction of new galleries for the Department of European Sculpture and Decorative Arts in the Henry R. Kravis Wing and the Carroll and Milton Petrie European Sculpture Court in 1990, the physical expansion of the Museum—its footprint in the Park, so to speak—has come to a close.

The Petrie Court, much like the Blumenthal Patio, which opened in 1964, was intended as an *aire de repos* and serves as a display area for French and Italian seventeenth- and eighteenth-century outdoor statuary, set amidst the rich and varied collections of European decorative arts. Through its glass west wall the visitor can look out on a changing seasonal scene that features Cleopatra's Needle, the obelisk of Thutmosis III. Within the court the natural light is not only refreshing but also illuminates the marble sculptures placed in the court, changing in a way gallery lighting cannot. It is a favorite spot for students and artists, who spend much time there with sketch pads. As with the Lehman Wing, which retained the original 1880 neo-Gothic granite and red-brick Park façade, the Petrie Court incorporates the Museum's 1888 Italianate south façade and carriage entrance, also of granite and red brick, as its north wall.

In order to minimize the sliverlike proportions of the tall, narrow space, Kevin Roche worked closely with Olga Raggio, Iris and B. Gerald Cantor Chairman of the Department of European Sculpture and Decorative Arts, and developed an arcaded south wall, inspired by the Orangerie of Versailles, with a number of pronounced horizontal elements and a win-

dow at the east end cut into the corridor of the Robert Wood Johnson Jr. Gallery for works on paper. The window has a dual purpose: first, to provide a stunning, plunging view onto the court; and second, to let much-needed light into the narrow corridor above. During the recent renovation of the Johnson Gallery, contractors uncovered a neo-Gothic arch from the Museum's original 1880 Fifth Avenue façade, which had been walled over when Richard Howland Hunt completed the Great Hall in 1902. The arch will be left exposed as a further memento of the Museum's history.

Among the sculptures in the Petrie Court are two imposing term figures of Priapus and Flora, executed in 1616 for the

Opposite: The Carroll and Milton Petrie European Sculpture Court

*Above: Tour group with Houdon's **Bather** in the center of the court*

Below: Neo-Gothic arch from the Museum's Fifth Avenue façade, by Calvert Vaux, 1872–80. Uncovered during renovation of the Robert Wood Johnson Jr. Gallery, 1992

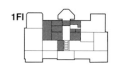

1Fl

Villa Borghese in Rome by Gian Pietro Bernini, father of Gian Lorenzo Bernini, whose early *Faun Teased by Children* is displayed nearby; all three were bought, entirely or in part, with Annenberg funds. The focus of the center of the court is Houdon's marvelous marble *Bather*. At the south side, in the arcade along the edge of the Kravis Wing, is our distinguished collection of French and Italian seventeenth- and eighteenth-century portrait busts, among which are those of Samuel Bernard, Louis XIV's banker, by Guillaume Coustou, and Mme de Pompadour, mistress and confidante of Louis XV, by Jean-Baptiste Pigalle.

The new first-floor galleries for European sculpture and decorative arts in the Kravis Wing have made possible a comprehensive installation of works from the Renaissance to the beginning of the twentieth century. Just south of the Petrie Court is the Josephine Bay Paul Gallery (1990) devoted primarily to French eighteenth-century sculpture, ranging from three large reliefs by Clodion made for the Hôtel de

Above: Faun Teased by Children, by Gian Lorenzo Bernini, Italian. Marble, ca. 1616–17. Purchase, The Annenberg Fund, Inc. Gift, Fletcher, Rogers and Louis V. Bell Funds, and Gift of J. Pierpont Morgan, by exchange, 1976

Center: Sketching in the arcade of the Petrie Court

Bourbon-Condé in Paris to small terracotta models, including one of our most recent acquisitions, *Venus and Cupid*, the only *bozzetto*, or sketch, by the great Neo-classical Italian sculptor Antonio Canova in an American collection.

Adjacent to the Paul Gallery is the latest of our new spaces in the Kravis Wing, the Florence Gould Galleries, inaugurated in 1993. Among the highlights of these galleries, arranged in four stylistic groupings,

Baroque, Rococo, Neoclassical, and Empire, are a pair of magnificent Baroque marble portrait busts by Giovanni Battista Foggini of Cosimo III de' Medici and his elder son, Ferdinando, purchased with funds from the Annenberg Foundation.

Nineteenth-century works in many media are housed in the galleries adjoining Gould that opened in 1991. These are named in honor of their donors, Iris and B. Gerald Cantor, to whom we also owe Rodin's magnificent *Burghers of Calais*, the most monu-

western, or Central Park, side of the Museum, a prime objective of the Master Plan. Visitors can now pass easily from the American Wing or arms and armor or the arts of Africa to the Wallace Wing without going through the Great Hall. By diverting the flow of some public traffic away from the Great Hall, we avoid overcrowding and also encourage visits to previously less-frequented sections of the permanent collections.

Although not specifically addressed in the Master Plan, there are several galleries for European sculpture and decorative arts that have been added within the building in the last twenty years. Much of this extensive installation activity was spurred by the need to put on view single works of art or major collections, such as the Untermyer and Sheafer furniture—too long relegated to storage—and to accommodate a number of major recent acquisitions, many made possible by friends of the department. Among the most spectacular of these are the superlative and extensive French interiors and furnishings of the eighteenth century, all gifts from Charles and Jayne Wrightsman's private collection, which form the core of the twelve beautifully appointed period rooms in the Wrightsman Galleries, the first of which opened in 1969 and the last in 1989. Strolling

mental of their Rodin gifts, many of which are exhibited in the new Nineteenth-Century European Paintings and Sculpture Galleries (see p. 65). The Iris and B. Gerald Cantor Galleries were created to meet the needs of our increasing activity in acquisitions of European nineteenth-century decorative arts, and they are now installed with all the vitrines filled.

However, we should consider these holdings still in their infancy. The space itself cannot be expanded, but eventually we may expect the collections to be improved qualitatively. This is because—and it is clearly evident from this text—a museum is never finished and collections can always be refined and expanded. Furthermore, in opening galleries in a new field, we are encouraging interest in that field and, as a result, spurring curators into acquiring more deliberately and also attracting collectors, who often become donors only after the Museum has demonstrated a commitment to their field.

The recently constructed galleries on the first floor of the Kravis Wing and the Petrie Court created a new north-south axis along the

Above: Room from the Palais Paar, Vienna. Designed by Isidor Canevale (1730–1786). Opposite: Room from the Hôtel de Varengeville, Paris, about 1735. Acquired with funds given by Mr. and Mrs. Charles Wrightsman, 1963

Right: The Marriage Feast at Cana, by Juan de Flandes, Flemish. Oil on wood, ca. 1500. The Jack and Belle Linsky Collection, 1982

from the shopfront of 3, quai Bourbon, in a circuit that takes you past Sèvres porcelains, the Varengeville, Paar, and Cabris rooms to the de Tessé salon that once overlooked the Seine, and on across the hall to the bedroom in the style of Louis XIV, one can survey a full century of French interiors and decorations at their very highest level.

The standards of excellence that prevailed in every aspect of the installation of these rooms have also guided the Wrightsmans' acquisitions of European paintings, and much of their spectacular collection has already been given to the Museum. Masterpiece after masterpiece in our galleries, from Vermeer to Rubens to J. L. David, bear the

Wrightsman credit line, as do numerous purchases made from the Wrightsman Fund for Western European arts, established by Jayne Wrightsman in 1985.

Jack and Belle Linsky's collection, given to the Museum in 1982, was one of New York's choicest in fine French eighteenth-century furniture, Renaissance bronzes, European cabinet-sized pictures, and various categories of decorative arts, with special strengths in Russian eighteenth- and nineteenth-century porcelain as well as in Renaissance jewelry. The Linskys' taste favored small, highly precious, and refined objects. It was their wish that the collection be shown as a unit, a display restriction that often makes it

The Salon in The Jack and Belle Linsky Galleries, 1984. Furnishings are primarily 18th-century French.

difficult for a museum to present the history of art to its visitors in a clear and coherent manner. However, in the case of the Linsky gift, with the exception of the paintings, which are a bit removed from the main second-floor paintings galleries, the rest of the collection relates well to the neighboring galleries of bronzes, porcelains, and furniture.

Also on the first floor, we continued our efforts at systematic presentation of all of our European sculpture and decorative arts by opening the department's first permanent installation of Central European works. It was funded by Jayne Wrightsman and Mr. and Mrs. John H. Gutfreund. The Gutfreunds also funded the French Renaissance Gallery, which was completed last year. Here we have installed an imposing limestone fireplace, a gift from the William Randolph Hearst Foundation and the Hearst Foundation, Inc., as well as our great tapestries from Château d'Anet, woven for Henri II's mistress, Diane de Poitiers.

Across the Tapestry Hall to the north and leading to our arms and armor collection, with which it opened concurrently, is a gallery for Italian sixteenth-century sculpture and decorative arts. This gallery enables us to show for the first time a 1971 acquisition, our tall gray-sandstone wall fountain, carved about 1528 by the Florentine Simone Mosca.

Quite appropriately, in October 1993, the Department of European Sculpture and Decorative Arts also completed its move into the Museum's first compact art-storage space. This facility, designed to house over 20,000 objects in 9,500 square feet, replaces nine dispersed, outdated storerooms that had taken up 13,000 square feet. The new area features a rolling-carriage system of shelves and drawers on tracks—a dense but flexible and accessible storage arrangement that has led to an orderly and easy-to-use organization of the collection.

Another major occupant of the new space created in the Kravis Wing is the Sherman Fairchild Center for Objects Conservation, named to honor Sherman Fairchild, who died in 1971. Opened in 1992, the center houses the largest of our conservation departments, with responsibility for more than 200,000 works of art—including all sculpture,

Clockwise:
In the French Renaissance Gallery, fireplace, 1st quarter of the 16th century. Gift of William Randolph Hearst Foundation and The Hearst Foundation, Inc., 1977

Detail of tapestry of The Drowning of Britomartis, probably Paris, 1547–59. Gift of the children of Mrs. Harry Payne Whitney, 1942

Wall fountain, by Simone Mosca, Italian. Ca. 1528. Harris Brisbane Dick Fund, 1971

metalwork, glass, ceramics, furniture, and archaeological artifacts. The opening of this facility follows by twelve years the completion in the main building of the Sherman Fairchild Paintings Conservation Center. With the addition of these spaces, two magnificent facilities for treatment and research, and the forthcoming completion of the Antonio Ratti Textile Center we will have made significant progress in our major campaign to modernize and expand our conservation departments, which, as recognized by the Master Plan, were badly in need of updating. The Paper Conservation Laboratory should also be modernized and given more space, and plans for the relocation and improvement of the Asian Conservation Laboratory are now on the drawing board.

It should be noted that conservation has changed dramatically at the Met since the early 1900s, when our curators undertook cleaning and repairs themselves. In the course of this century, not only has that practice become a thing of the past, with conservation assumed by fully trained conservators, but techniques have become increasingly more scientific and our departments more specialized. Also, the scope of the field has considerably broadened as new methods and technology enable us to study the structure of an object, and art-historical questions are now frequently answered through the collaborative investigations of curators and conservators. Well-equipped, modernized laboratories are thus essential for new analytical techniques to provide these insights, as well as to conduct the most appropriate treatments for the preservation of works of art.

The Arms and Armor Galleries were totally refurbished in a long campaign that received great encouragement from Board Chairman Arthur Ochs Sulzberger, who contributed generously and also, through his love of the field, provided the requisite leadership. Others, among them collector Ronald Lauder, the Annie Laurie Aitken Charitable Trust, Robert M. Lee and the Hunting World Group of Companies, and the Japanese business community (through the Japan Foundation), also donated funds for the project, which took four years to complete. This interval allowed us to clean and restore many objects in the collection as well as the architectural elements of the 1910 Pierpont Morgan Wing itself, which has housed arms and armor since 1956. Among the highlights of this renovation were the first major installation in more than fifty years of our renowned Japanese arms and armor collection, the finest outside Japan, and new settings for a number of spectacular acquisitions since 1972, including the Louis XIII flintlock hunting gun acquired that year; the child's armor for the future Louis I of Spain dating to 1712, acquired in 1989; and the sumptuous Turkish sword from the workshop of the court of Süleyman the Magnificent, acquired in 1993.

Other important changes that marked the reopening of the galleries were subtle but substantive in terms of scholarly accuracy. These included extensive conservation on a number of pieces, notably some late-fifteenth-century German shields, from which as many as five layers of paint were cleaned to recover their original emblems. We also used this opportunity to remove inappropriate modern elements from some of the knights' armors of the central equestrian group.

Above: The Arms and Armor Galleries, reinstalled 1991

Left: Japanese armor, late Kamakura period, early 14th century. Gift of Bashford Dean, 1914

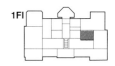

59

Our Arms and Armor Galleries, with their outstanding examples from Europe, Asia, the Americas, and the Islamic world have always been one of the memorable experiences for visitors of all ages, who may now, from this much more inclusive installation, get a truly universal sense of the beauty and fine craftsmanship lavished on weaponry over the centuries.

Beauty and fine craftsmanship are also lavished on another category of objects not primarily associated with the visual arts, musical instruments. Though these are richly represented at the Metropolitan, it was not until 1971 that they were properly displayed in galleries funded by the widow of the noted music impresario André Mertens, in whose honor they are named. The core of the collection was formed by donations made by Mrs. John Crosby Brown, starting in 1884 and extending over a quarter of a century. Her gifts are broad in their representation, reaching across the globe and including instruments that range from the most modest in provenance to the most courtly. Research, restoration, and performance amplify the collection's purpose, and

visitors to the Mertens Galleries may appreciate the visual qualities of the instruments and enjoy as well a variety of musical experiences.

During the 1980s, which were the years of the most intense construction for the Master Plan, the Department of Medieval Art went ahead with several projects. In 1982–83 two new galleries were inaugurated in the main building. The first was the reinstalled Medieval Treasury, made possible through the support of former Chairman of the Board J. Richardson Dilworth. The second was the newly established Lawrence A. and Barbara Fleischman Gallery of Late Medieval Secular Art, featuring objects of daily use, many of which had not been previously exhibited.

The Cloisters celebrated its fiftieth anniversary in 1988 with the redesign of its Treasury, made possible by Hélène and Michel David-Weill. This gallery houses small and precious works such as illuminated manuscripts, silver-gilt and jeweled reliquaries, and other liturgical objects. It also includes the brilliantly carved Bury Saint Edmunds cross and two magnificent books of hours, those of Jeanne d'Evreux and Jean, duke of Berry, as well as textiles for the first time, protected by more advanced light and climate control in their new surroundings.

Above: German jousting armor, ca. 1580–90. Gift of Henry G. Keasbey, 1926

Above right: Violins in The André Mertens Galleries for Musical Instruments, opened 1971

Center: Child's armor, French, dated 1712. Purchase, Armand Hammer, Occidental Petroleum Corporation Gift, 1989

Map left to right: Islamic, Ancient Near Eastern, and Musical Instruments galleries

2Fl

ing, and improved offices and storage areas for the department.

In 1980, as the first stage in the reinstallation of the Ancient Near Eastern collection, we created the Raymond and Beverly Sackler Gallery for Assyrian Art. This gallery shows our impressive series of ninth-century B.C. reliefs and the human-headed lion and bull in a "court" arrangement that reflects the original architecture

Left: The Cloisters Treasury, redesigned in 1988 with funds provided by Hélène and Michel David-Weill

The entire Fifth Avenue side of the Museum, north and south of the Great Hall, has retained its original geographical organization, with Greek and Roman, Ancient Near Eastern, and Islamic art to the south and Egyptian and Asian to the north. Early on during the Master Plan, in 1975, we relocated and completely renovated our Islamic galleries, in which miniatures, carpets, glass, ceramics, and jewelry are displayed together. The galleries are the setting for another architectural element taken into our care, the richly decorated Nur al-Din Room, built as the reception area for a house in Damascus in 1707. These galleries, nearly twenty years old, have stood up remarkably well, both physically and conceptually. Still, some changes are contemplated that include a new, more welcoming entrance, better light-

of the palace of Ashurnasirpal II at Nimrud. New galleries for Iranian and Mesopotamian art were thereafter opened in 1984, thanks to James N. Spears and the Hagop Kevorkian and Dillon funds. Additional space was provided this year on an interim basis for the art of Anatolia, the Levant, and the eastern Mediterranean world, in a gallery funded by Raymond and Beverly Sackler. Later, as part of the Greek and Roman building project, these Ancient Near Eastern galleries will be entirely redone, as the installation of climate-control systems will require substantial demolition.

Above: In the Raymond and Beverly Sackler Gallery for Assyrian Art, winged lion and bull from the palace of Ashurnasirpal II, Nimrud. 883–859 B.C. Gift of John D. Rockefeller Jr., 1932

Left: Nur al-Din Room, Syrian, 1707, in the Islamic galleries. Gift of the Kevorkian Foundation, 1970

Building from Within

As we have seen in these pages, the Master Plan was an evolving process allowing for a number of changes caused by many factors, not least of which was the reexamination of museological issues. This review prompted, for example, such major steps as the building of the Wallace Wing for twentieth-century art and, on a lesser scale, conversion of the Johnson Gallery into an area for rotating displays of works on paper (see p. 65). Meanwhile, growth of collections drove the creation of new installations such as the Irving Galleries for the Arts of South and Southeast Asia and the Jan Mitchell Treasury for Precolumbian gold. A greater emphasis on conservation mandated the Sherman Fairchild Center for Objects Conservation, and the need for better access and management of our extensive textile holdings prompted the soon-to-open Antonio Ratti Textile Center (see p. 76).

Some changes made to the galleries in the last few years have been more subtle but equally significant. One such example is the renovation of the Great Hall second-floor balcony, thanks to a grant from Stanley Herzman, who also gave the Museum the majority of his fine collection of Chinese porcelains. This project called for a more comprehensive chronological display of our Asian ceramics, primarily Chinese; for a more rigorous selection, with greater emphasis on absolutely the finest quality; and for more stress on earlier periods, reflecting current taste and collecting patterns. The presentation also aimed for greater spareness and, with the use of advanced lighting technology, such as fiber optics, has achieved much-improved illumination of the handsomely decorated undersides of many of the pieces. Furthermore, the formerly stark, rectilinear exhibition cases were brought into conformance with the Beaux-Arts vocabulary of Richard Morris Hunt's Great Hall through the addition of appropriately detailed base and cornice moldings. Over time, of course, this installation will itself change—as most do at the Metropolitan—not only to accommodate new acquisitions but to further enhance

*Opposite: In the Nineteenth-Century European Paintings and Sculpture Galleries, **The Bronze Age**, by Auguste Rodin, French. Cast ca. 1906. Gift of Mrs. John W. Simpson, 1907*

Above: Galleries during construction

Asian ceramics, including those from the Herzman and Altman collections (left), are exhibited on the renovated Great Hall balcony (above).

The Temple of Dendur before and after removal of the parapet's top course. Now in place are two colossi of Amenhotep III, from the Temple

of Luxor, Thebes. Dynasty 18, ca. 1391–1353 B.C. Rogers Fund and Edward S. Harkness Gift, 1921

inconsequential changes in this area. As I have already mentioned, we made the first inner chamber accessible with minor physical alterations of steps and a ramp. This initiative has been joyfully received by our visitors, who were long frustrated by the forbidding—and forbidden—granite platform separating them from what are among the finest reliefs anywhere on the temple. Nearby, several purchases and a gift of over a hundred Amarna reliefs from Mr. and Mrs. Jonathan Rosen have led to an installation on the south wall of the temple enclosure that enlivens this rather stark surface. Stark as well, we felt, were the vast stone expanses surrounding the temple, and Dorothea Arnold, Lila Acheson Wallace Curator in Charge, has given the adjacent space greater interest and life through the addition of the superb reliefs from the Chapel of Ramesses I at Abydos, thanks to a grant from the Malcolm Hewitt Wiener Foundation, Inc., and the placement of a number of sculptures, notably a group of monumental Sakhmet statues, along the east wall.

Still further improvement to the Temple of Dendur area was made this summer, when we removed the top course of the tribune's granite parapet, which had served as a bench back but also, unfortunately, as a massive visual barrier to the temple.

our knowledge of ceramics by showing particular developments such as the influence of Asian porcelain in the West, as seen in Chinese Export or in Delft Blue and White.

The Museum's increasing concern for public access to the collections caused us to cast a fresh eye on the Temple of Dendur and to undertake small but not

A growing desire for more regular and expanded displays of certain elements of the Met's collections, heretofore presented only in the context of special exhibitions, led to the creation of newly configured galleries for costumes and for works on paper. For years, under the inspired leadership of the late Diana Vreeland, the Costume Institute mounted one major exhibition each year, combining works from the collection with loans. Eventually, as conservation standards in the field imposed ever more severe restrictions to reduce exposure of the costumes to light, the "downtime" between the yearly Costume Institute shows increased to six months or more each year. Recognizing that we could not afford to have so much prime space dark and unused for long periods, nor to keep so much of our extensive collection off view, we decided to redesign the gallery space to make it possible—and affordable— to mount three somewhat smaller exhibitions every year, thereby using the richness of our holdings more creatively and keeping costumes on view year-round. Curator in Charge Richard Martin and Associate Curator Harold Koda have implemented this policy since January 1993 with tremendous success.

The principle of making collections of light-sensitive works of art such as costumes available by frequent rotations has now been applied to works on paper with the conversion in 1993 of the Robert Wood Johnson Jr. Recent Acquisitions Gallery into a space for the continual display of drawings, prints, and photographs. All three of these media are ones in which the Metropolitan has vast, absolutely superb holdings, from which remarkably little has been shown regularly.

Indeed, until 1993 works on paper had been shown in periodic thematic or monographic exhibitions, often focused on only one of these media, with the result that visitors could not be certain whether any drawings, prints, or photographs would be on view the day they came to the Museum. This serious disservice, both to the museum-goer and to the collections, has now been happily rectified, thanks to funds from the Drue Heinz Foundation and the Bodman and Achelis foundations; and it is a joy to see our audience captivated by these marvelous, intimate works of art in the carpeted and com-

fortable Johnson Gallery. Furthermore, because this gallery is on the main axis leading from the European Paintings Galleries to the new Nineteenth-Century Galleries, many who might not ordinarily seek out drawings, prints, and photographs now find themselves deriving great pleasure from them.

The most important recent gallery change in the building was the renovation of the spaces for nineteenth-century European paintings and sculpture. Unlike the projects just described, which were subtle by comparison, this involved a far more drastic decision, to tear down and redo ab initio a major installation opened within the period under review.

Above top: "Waist Not," an exhibition in the new Costume Institute, Mar. 29– Aug. 21, 1994

Above bottom: The Robert Wood Johnson Jr. Gallery for works on paper. Renovation supported by the Drue Heinz Foundation and the Bodman and Achelis foundations

Old and new — Nineteenth-Century European Paintings and Sculpture Galleries

Manet works, formerly in separate spaces, are now concentrated in one large gallery.

Inefficient use of space and multiple vistas have been replaced by more wall area and a coherent presentation.

Our reasons for taking this dramatic step reflected a profound change at the Museum in the way of presenting European—mostly French—paintings and sculptures of the nineteenth century. Our radically new approach was born of a happy convergence of viewpoints, my own and that of Engelhard Curator Gary Tinterow.

When the vast space that would be devoted to these collections was originally built in 1972, as the second floor of the incomplete Rockefeller Wing, Sir John Pope-Hennessy, then chairman of the European Paintings department, wanted to exploit the open, clear-span 200-by-120-foot area. Accordingly, he devised a scheme of free-floating partitions that could be placed in almost any configuration, providing, as seemed the order of the day in a number of museums around the world, great flexibility. The bright expanse of daylight and the multiple vistas onto one great Impressionist and Post-Impressionist picture after another were at first sight dazzling. In the end, however, the arrangement proved confusing. The partitions on which the paintings were hung also had a provisional look and turned out not to be as flexible as intended—in fact they were never moved. And, most seriously, the walls did not allow for a hanging scheme that would do justice to the strengths of the collection, namely, its constellations of works by individual artists such as Degas or Manet, and there was no room for growth, although many paintings were acquired in the 1980s.

Therefore in 1989 it was decided that this space should be redesigned, and in 1991, when Walter Annenberg announced the anticipated bequest to the Metropolitan of his fabulous collection of Impressionists and Post-Impressionists, the timing was perfect. We were able to adjust the plans so that the Annenberg Collection could be shown, as he requested, as a unit in the midst of our own holdings.

Our principal goal in redoing the galleries was to provide a more coherent presentation of the collections by expanding the available wall space and creating a setting that we felt was more in keeping with what the nineteenth-century artists might themselves have envisioned for their works—a Beaux-Arts rather than a contemporary style. The result is a suite of classically proportioned galleries that incorporates architectural details adapted from designs done by McKim, Mead and White for the Metropolitan early in this century. These rooms are in harmony not only with the art they contain but with the main Museum building itself.

The galleries honor donors both past and present who supported their construction, including Walter Annenberg, Janice H. Levin, and Iris and B. Gerald Cantor, as well as André Meyer, whose gift in 1972 helped the Museum to build the space the galleries now occupy. At the inaugural installation we were able to display the fifty-three works from the Annenberg Collection as well as Impressionist pictures that were made promised or partial gifts by a number of other generous patrons, including paintings from Mr. and Mrs. Douglas Dillon and Janice Levin, and a group of sculptures by Rodin from the Iris and B. Gerald Cantor Foundation. We also unveiled additional works acquired with Annenberg funds, two major paintings by Vincent van Gogh: *Shoes*, a deeply moving work of 1888, and *Wheat Field with Cypresses*, a masterpiece of the Arles period. As of this writing, 1.7 million visitors have enjoyed these new galleries, and their response to the redesign has been overwhelmingly favorable.

Above: 19th-century sculptures include Rodin's Study for the Monument to Balzac. *Bronze, modeled 1897; cast 1972. Gift of Iris and B. Gerald Cantor Foundation, 1984*

Left: Van Gogh's Wheat Field with Cypresses *(at left), Purchase, The Annenberg Foundation Gift, 1993, next to the artist's* Olive Orchard, *from the collection of Walter H. and Leonore Annenberg*

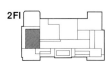

Building for the Future

While this publication has documented through text and image the full extent of building and reconfiguration at the Metropolitan since 1970, it also cannot fail to have shown that much remains to be done. After twenty-seven years at the Met, sixteen of them as director, I feel I can safely say that at least the broad outlines of future space needs and allocations within the existing building are now fairly well determined. For one, we now know precisely how much space we have for our use on this site. For another, our collecting process has matured to the point where it seems unlikely that we would receive many gifts that would have the institution-wide impact of the 1969 Michael C. Rockefeller Memorial Collection, which so dramatically altered the mix of civilizations presented by the Metropolitan.

I make such a prediction with some hesitation, being mindful of having written in the 1978 *Annual Report* that "the previous decade's range of achievement in acquisitions, in special exhibitions and programs, in the construction of new wings and in the reinstallation of galleries was of a magnitude that will not and cannot be matched." Clearly, this prediction was wide of the mark, for, amazingly enough, the pace of activity in the next fifteen years turned out not to have slowed down one bit, not in construction, not in the number and scale of special exhibitions, and not even in the area of acquisitions—witness the Jack and Belle Linsky Collection in 1982 and the anticipated bequest of the Annenberg Collection announced in 1991. Nor is the pace in most of these areas about to diminish. Still, we can now see ahead, across the coming decade, to the completion

of most of our planned major gallery installations and support facilities—to the realization of most of the 1970 Master Plan, or, to borrow Catherine de Médicis' term, our "grand dessein." Those were her words to describe the Louvre's own master plan, initiated in 1565 as a royal palace and only now nearing its final phase as a museum as part of the Grand Louvre project. I am optimistic that our own Master Plan will be finished in a somewhat shorter span of time!

At this stage of our planning for the future it is striking to see how close we are to the ultimate goal of achieving our great encyclopedia of world art. I should add that unlike the Master Plan, which was based largely on the addition of entire wings, our new ventures constitute building strictly from within, as we are circumscribed by our existing perimeter in the park. Thus expansion in one area calls for a reexamination of priorities, as the gain of a square foot anywhere means a corresponding loss elsewhere or considerable ingenuity—and expense—in the capturing of unused spaces such as air shafts or attics high above galleries, which do not project beyond the present silhouette of the building.

Our most ambitious project for the future will be the comprehensive review and reinstallation of the Greek and Roman collections, numbering some 35,000 works of art and archaeological materials. This project is already in the planning stages, and a generous leadership gift from collectors Robert and Renée Belfer has just been received.

Other significant projects are also either in the planning stages or in progress, and I would like to address them first. They are of enormous importance in fulfilling our objective of placing all of our major works of art on view—conserving them and making them readily accessible to the public according to the most appropriate means available.

One of the largest of these projects, already far advanced, is the completion of the spaces for Asian art, creating on the second floor at the north end of the building a vast new museum within the Museum. This area will eventually consist of a set of offices, storage areas, and galleries comprising 75,000 square feet, which will constitute, in effect, the largest Asian art museum in the Western world.

I have already mentioned the completion of the Great Hall balcony for Asian ceramics and of the Weber Galleries for the Arts of Ancient China. The Arts of Japan Galleries, which have proven to be a versatile and apt setting for our collections, may also be considered "finished"—for now—and, of course,

Below: Carroll and Milton Petrie European Sculpture Court and Lila Acheson Wallace Wing

we have just opened the Irving Galleries for the Arts of South and Southeast Asia. At present, of our small collection of Korean art only the ceramics are on view on the Great Hall balcony. Clearly, some day a proper space must be devoted to this important culture. This leaves only our extensive Chinese holdings to be attended to, and quite

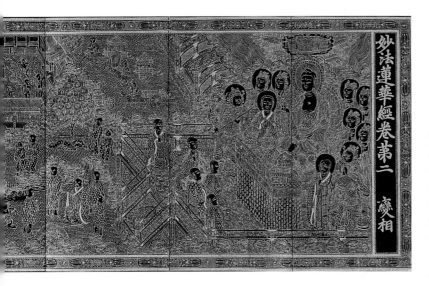

妙法蓮華經卷第二 變相

Illustrated Lotus Sutra, Korean. Koryo period, ca. 1340. Gold and silver on indigo-dyed paper. Purchase, Lila Acheson Wallace Gift, 1994

a bit of new thinking has informed how we are to proceed.

The Dillon Galleries for Chinese painting, which opened in 1981, have served us and the field very well, providing a regular rotation of works from the permanent collection and, through numerous special exhibitions, notably "Iron-Wire Line: Chinese Figure Painting" (1985) and "Mountains of the Mind: Nature and Self in Early Chinese Landscape Painting" (1988–89), the whole range of Chinese painting from the Sung through the Ch'ing dynasty (960–1911). In the last few years our collection of Chinese paintings has reached a level now worthy of the Metropolitan, and prices have climbed so steadily that further purchases are likely to be, at most, intermittent. Our focus has now shifted to a heretofore underemphasized yet important aspect of Chinese culture, the decorative arts. The initiative in this direction has been led by Senior Curator James Watt and by Florence and Herbert Irving, whose collecting interests have proven very broad indeed.

It also became clear as we reviewed the overall plan of the Chinese galleries that their sequence has to be made more logical. Because the galleries do not connect at the north, the flow from the Sung and Yüan dynasties (960–1368) to the Ming and Ch'ing (1368–1911) is interrupted. By incorporating the north gallery, formerly used for special exhibitions, into the sequence of galleries, we will achieve the link between these dynasties and provide as well the requisite space for the inclusion of Chinese paintings of the nineteenth and twentieth centuries, richly represented thanks to the 1986 gift from Robert Ellsworth.

Moreover, we now feel that the time has come to integrate decorative arts into the display of painting and calligraphy, an approach that more correctly reflects the original historical context of many of these works and also provides a more varied and dynamic presentation. Therefore in the redesign of the Chinese paintings galleries, which will be extended across the north gallery in a continuous U shape, furniture, jades, and ceramics, principally, will be incorporated with painting and calligraphy, a concept successfully introduced in our Arts of Japan Galleries. Where works by literati painters are shown, the display will include some antiquities collected by them. In contrast to our Nineteenth-Century Paintings and Sculpture Galleries, however, where we have been able to evoke the Beaux-Arts style of the period, it would be impossible for us to re-create Chinese architectural settings appropriate to the various dynasties represented.

Douglas Dillon, as a further expression of support for the Museum and with a truly amazing élan of generosity, has also donated substantial funds to the redesign and expansion of the galleries named in his honor. The remainder of that space will bear the name of Oscar Tang, in memory of Frances Young Tang. Oscar Tang has made this renovation possible and along with Jack C. Tang has given us major Chinese paintings, most notably Li Kung-lin's *The Classic of Filial Piety* from the P. Y. and Kinmay W. Tang Family Collection.

Taking advantage of the height of the old north gallery, we will transect it and build a new third floor devoted exclusively to Chinese decorative arts from the Sung through the Ch'ing dynasty. (Pre-Sung antiquities are located in the Weber Galleries.) One of the two main rooms on this third floor will be devoted to the Museum's collection of Chinese lacquer, to be greatly augmented by the promised gift of the Irvings' Asian collection. Once again the Irvings have also provided the funds for the installation and the gallery, which will bear their names. The other large room will be reserved for special exhibitions, but both will be designed to accommodate periodic shows of our extensive holdings of Chinese costumes and textiles, which are light-sensitive and cannot be put on view continually. A smaller gallery will become a home for the Bishop Collection of Chinese jade, and three others will be devoted to displays combining works in other media, such as bronze, enamel, bamboo, ivory, porcelain, and glass. We expect to open these galleries in early 1997, and with the exception of the Korean room our Asian museum will then be complete.

As I have pointed out earlier, however, the Metropolitan is a collection of many museums within a museum and not all of them are at the same stage of development. While in the not-too-distant future we can see the end point of our long campaign for our Asian collections, there are other parts of the Metropolitan where substantial renovations and installations are planned.

As we approach the Museum's 125th anniversary next year, we feel that a major and very visible statement about the building and the collections needs to be made, and to this end it seems natural to focus on the most prominent of our galleries, that at the top of the Grand Staircase where the Museum's preeminent collection of Tiepolo

Models of the new Chinese galleries, in which painting, calligraphy, and the decorative arts will be shown together. An elevator (at left in lower photo), providing additional access, will display a work of art and remain open when not in use.

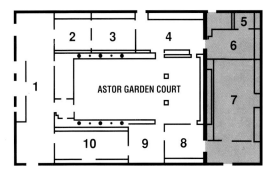

The Chinese galleries will incorporate the north gallery (shaded), formerly for special exhibitions, creating an uninterrupted sequence: 1. Astor forecourt; 2,3. Early–late Sung; 4. Yüan; 5. Textiles; 6,7. Ming; 8. Ch'ing; 9. Literati; 10. Late Ch'ing–20th century

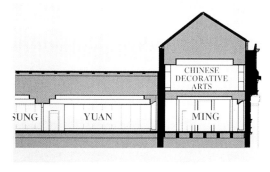

Cross section showing the third floor devoted to Chinese decorative arts

paintings is hung. At the moment the approach to this gallery, designated for Dr. Mortimer D. Sackler and Theresa Sackler, is marred by the unfortunate presence of a

Before and after views (shown in a model) of the paintings by Giovanni Battista Tiepolo for the Ca' Dolfin, Venice. The canvases will be reframed to conform to their original irregular shapes as set into the walls of the Venetian palace.

Far right: In June the pictures were temporarily hung in the Great Hall under the supervision of Keith Christiansen, Jayne Wrightsman Curator of European Paintings. In the background is **The Capture of Carthage,** *from Ca' Dolfin, 1726–30. Rogers Fund, 1965*

lunette that partially fills and thus diminishes the grandeur of the Richard Morris Hunt limestone arch and of the vista from below of one of the gigantic paintings executed by Giovanni Battista Tiepolo for the Ca' Dolfin, in Venice. In addition, our three largest canvases are squeezed between a low ceiling and the floor, which causes the central picture, the one seen from the Great Hall, to look almost crushed. Not only is this plainly ugly but it completely subverts any hope we may have of suggesting the nobility and high spaces of Tiepolo's original setting, a grand Baroque palace. Raising the ceiling and restoring the arch to its original state will require major construction that involves the roof and skylight, but as can be seen from the model (at left, center and bottom), it is well worth doing. And when we are able to proceed, it will be thanks to a generous grant from the Drue Heinz Foundation. (Mrs. Heinz is a trustee and chairman of the European Paintings Department Visiting Committee.)

It may come as a surprise to many of our readers that if asked what is our greatest single work of art of the Italian Renaissance we might name a consummate masterpiece that has not been on view for over three decades: the *studiolo* (or small private study) from the palace of Duke Federigo da Montefeltro at Gubbio, in Umbria (near Perugia). This *studiolo* is largely conceived in terms of its illusionistic wainscoting, in which trompe-l'oeil images were ingeniously executed in intarsia by a leading Florentine workshop of the fifteenth century. One of the finest of its type in existence, the *studiolo* is rivaled only by a similar illusionistic room still in situ in the ducal palace at Urbino. In late spring of 1996, after years of painstaking restoration, aided in part by the generosity of Board Vice-Chairman Annette de la Renta, we will reinstall the room in the first of the new Italian galleries, off the Medieval Hall, and stage an accompanying exhibition delineating the fascinating story of its technique and conservation. We are grateful to the Andrew W. Mellon Foundation for funding research and manuscript preparation for a forthcoming book on the *studiolo* by Olga Raggio and Conservator Antoine Wilmering.

Above: The Gubbio **studiolo**, *from Umbria, ca. 1476–80, will be reinstalled in late spring 1996. Conservator Antoine Wilmering (second from left) helps raise a panel in the conservation studio.*

Left: Ceiling being restored

The opening of the Gubbio *studiolo* is one of a number of projects aimed at completing the reinstallation of all of the holdings of the Department of European Sculpture and Decorative Arts. Among the others is the renovation of the English rooms begun with the Heathcote Gallery in 1987 and now under way in a series of spaces that will be designated for their sponsor, the Annie Laurie Aitken Charitable Trust.

Detail of panel from the Gubbio **studiolo**. *Rogers Fund, 1939*

Sketches for the Annie Laurie Aitken Galleries for English decorative arts include the state bed from Hampton Court, 1697–98. Gift of Mr. and Mrs. William Randolph Hearst Jr., 1968

Below: Nancy Britton (left), assistant conservator, supervises the bed's restoration.

In the new Aitken Galleries, our extensive collection of English decorative arts from the early seventeenth to the late eighteenth century will be shown in a setting that complements its quality and importance. Existing galleries will be remodeled with moldings and damask walls to provide period context for our Georgian furniture. The Kirtlington Park and Lansdowne House rooms will be repainted to match their original colors, which have been revealed through careful research, and the Tapestry Room from Croome Court will be cleaned and restored, thanks to the Samuel H. Kress Foundation. Furthermore, three new galleries will be created in a space previously used for furniture storage. One will contain the relocated Elizabethan Room from Great Yarmouth, Norfolk; the second, devoted to the late seventeenth century, will feature the great damask state bed from Hampton Court, Herefordshire; the third will include vitrines for our distinguished holdings of pottery, porcelain, and silver.

At a later date we will undertake a renovation and expansion of the Italian galleries, which have not existed as a coherent sequence since 1977, when they were displaced by an exhibition of the Irwin Untermyer collection of English furniture and the installation of the Elizabethan Room from Great Yarmouth. The relocation of these English collections to the Aitken Galleries and the conversion of a light well into a gallery will give us an opportunity to create a series of rooms devoted to the Italian Renaissance and Baroque periods, represented by important examples of fifteenth- to seventeenth-century sculpture and furniture, most acquired at the beginning of this century and not exhibited since the 1960s. In addition, the Renaissance decorative arts from northern Europe to be displaced by the Gubbio *studiolo* will be moved to the gallery now devoted to goldsmiths' work and scientific instruments, much of which will be retired to the department's new state-of-the-art storage facility.

Thus almost every space allotted to the Department of European Sculpture and Decorative Arts will have been reinstalled during the years between the late 1960s and late 1990s.

At this point, lest my text suggest that there are no flaws in all our grand schemes, I must note that while over the last few years European sculpture and decorative arts have indeed been given expanded and much-improved spaces, including the dramatic daylit Petrie Court, we are still not able to do full justice to this department's immensely rich holdings. Several important groups of objects will remain, at least for now, inadequately shown. Some of these compendia deserving more attention are the Hoentschel Collection of French woodwork given early in the century by J. Pierpont Morgan; the Baroque ivories collected by Mary Clark Thompson; the French silver bequeathed by Catherine D. Wentworth; the European ceramics carefully assembled by the late R. Thornton Wilson; and the Chinese porcelains made for European markets acquired over the years with funds from the Winfield Foundation.

I have written little up to now about one of the Museum's great strengths, medieval art, because we have no firm plans for a reinstallation of this department's collections, and a major renovation, in fact, may not be in order. Still, as much as we cherish our grand Medieval Hall and its austere yet inspiring appearance, it rather begs for a bit of change, such as the introduction of better lighting and of taller pedestals to show the sculptures at heights more in keeping with their original settings. Also, the so-called Byzantine corridor south of the Grand Staircase, where we display Byzantine and Migration art, contains perhaps more masterpieces and precious objects per square foot than any other part of the build-

The new Antonio Ratti Textile Center will replace poor storage and inade-quate work spaces.

Below: Elena Phipps packs tassles and then scans fabric with Florica Zaharia, conserva-tion assistant from the Cloisters.

Spring, Coptic. Wool and linen panel, ca. A.D. 400–450. Gift of George F. Baker Jr., 1890

addition of the north corridor to be vacated by the Department of Greek and Roman Art. The ancient silver displayed there is soon to be moved as part of that department's reinstallation. But before I address this renovation, the most ambitious and vast of our current capital projects, I would like to describe another major initiative with far-reaching implications for the Metropolitan and for the museum field at large, the Antonio Ratti Textile Center.

The Met houses one of the finest and most comprehensive collections of textiles in the world, second only perhaps to the Victoria and Albert Museum in London. Our more than 40,000 textiles come from every culture over three millennia and include such categories as tapestries, carpets, embroideries, lace, ecclesiastical vestments, and archaeological fragments. Whether Coptic or Tibetan, all are a precious summation of the iconographic and ornamental expressions of their civilizations, and, as such, they clearly represent a major component within the context of the Metropolitan. Here they are integrated with the other arts, and this manner of display is a major strength of this institution, for in

ing, but in a density surely detrimental to our appreciation of the material. The Attarouthi Treasure is among the more important acquisitions made in this area in recent years.

We plan to expand this space by the

drawn upon the resources of staff members of many departments, is to be inaugurated in December 1995.

By the time the Textile Center opens, we will have completed the planning stage of the largest and most ambitious of our projects for the future, the total renovation of the Greek and Roman Galleries; and indeed the first phase, the new Robert and Renée E. Belfer Court, will be only months away from opening.

most other museums textiles are isolated in specialized collections.

Although textiles require stringent environmental conditions for their preservation—they are highly vulnerable to the damage wrought by air, light, dirt, and repeated handling—they are stored in various departments around the building and are mostly inaccessible and in generally poor environmental surroundings. Likewise, conservation of textiles is now being conducted in several small studios, which are also inconveniently dispersed throughout the Museum. Clearly, this is a situation in urgent need of redress, and now, thanks to a major grant from the Fondazione Antonio Ratti, we are constructing on the ground level an over 25,000-square-foot study and storage facility and conservation laboratory, where almost all of our textiles will be brought together under optimum conditions with easy access for scholar, student, and layman alike.

The facility is intended to be up to date in every way, and we expect that it will be the largest and best-equipped textile center in any art museum. In order to provide easy access to the textiles and yet minimize their handling, images and information about all the pieces will be retrievable from computer monitors installed in a library and reference center. This immensely complex project, which has

The reinstallation of the Greek and Roman collections is an interesting manifestation of the nature of a large art museum, particularly of the cycles of taste and circumstance that mold it over time. An institution such as the Metropolitan is not born fully formed, as Athena from the brow of Zeus; rather, it grows by accretion, by the gradual or sometimes sudden and massive infusion of individual works of art or whole collections. An art

museum is shaped by willful acts and seren-dipities, as various trustees, donors, cura-tors, and directors with different interests and biases tug in one direction and then another. So it is that among the Met's first directors were archaeologists, di Cesnola and Edward Robinson in the classi-cal field and Herbert Winlock in the Egyptian. Little wonder that it was mainly during the first half of this museum's his-tory that the bulk of our objects in these fields were acquired, albeit aided by the then propitious climate for the acquisition of ancient art; when the laws of partage were still in effect, the Museum shared the discov-eries at its excavations with local departments of antiquities.

In other areas, such as Asian art, growth came later, as we have seen, because of the concerted interests of various individuals dur-ing the 1970s. There are further parallels in all fields at the Metropolitan, and it is because we are so large, so universal, and so mature that over time the landscape of our collections has evened out; for example, when one cura-tor's interest lay heavily in one area, his or her successor generally tipped the balance in another. Hence our collections are, as we often describe them, remarkably well balanced and broadly synoptic in all fields. Inevitably, though, a number of peaks and val-leys still give them a distinct character.

Long off view, works such as these will be shown in the new galleries.
*Above: **Emperor Augustus**, cameo. Roman, A.D. 41–54. Purchase, Joseph Pulitzer Bequest, 1942. Right top: Glass signed by Ennion as maker. Roman, 1st century A.D. Vase: Gift of Henry G. Marquand, 1881; cup and jug: Gift of J. Pierpont Morgan, 1917. Right: **Terracotta Actors**. Greek, proba-bly 4th century B.C. Rogers Fund, 1913. Below: **Triton and Tritoness**, gold arm bands. Probably north-ern Greece, ca. 200 B.C. Rogers Fund, 1956*

No institution as large as ours will ever have the staff, the financial resources, or even the time to do all that needs to be done simultaneously. Each task has to be under-taken at the right moment, and now that most of the Master Plan is close to comple-tion, we can turn once again to our "first love" and address the reinstallation of our extensive holdings of Greek and Roman art. This is a complex plan not unlike that of the reinstallation of the Wallace Galleries for

Egyptian art, and it is very similar in size and scope, both in the number of objects and in the number of square feet. Kevin Roche John Dinkeloo and Associates continue their work as the Museum's architects for this project.

The project is made more formidable because of the difficult logistical problems we confront in returning to the Greek and Roman department the space now occupied by the public restaurant and cafeteria, a space that had been devoted to Roman art until 1949. Sadly, ever since, the magnificent holdings of this department, especially metalwork, glass, terracottas, and engraved gems, have largely been off view, and too much of the art that has been displayed was crowded into galleries that were left unimproved because of other Museum priorities. This has been a source of frustration to Dietrich von Bothmer, who was head of the Greek and Roman department from 1959 to 1990—he

had joined it in 1946—and is now that department's first Distinguished Research Curator. We owe to Dr. von Bothmer, the greatest authority on Greek vases of his time, the acquisition, among others, of the calyx-krater by Euphronios representing Sleep and Death lifting the body of Sarpedon, arguably the finest red-figured vase in America.

Now the time has come for a complete

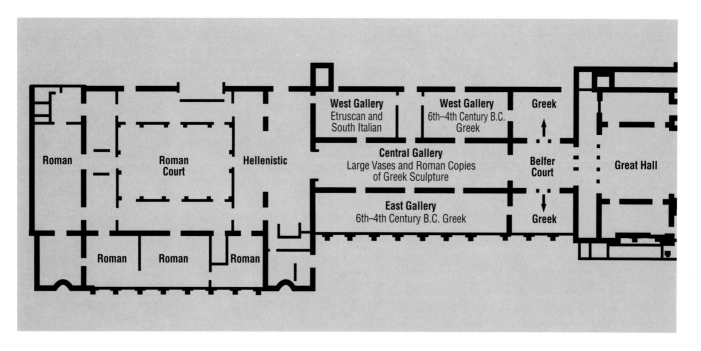

West Gallery
Etruscan and
South Italian

West Gallery
6th–4th Century B.C.
Greek

Greek

Roman

Roman
Court

Hellenistic

Central Gallery
Large Vases and Roman Copies
of Greek Sculpture

Belfer
Court

Great Hall

East Gallery
6th–4th Century B.C. Greek

Greek

Roman

Roman

Roman

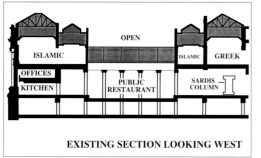

Proposal for new spaces for Greek and Roman art includes returning the public restaurant and cafeteria to the department (as shown in the cross section below), which had used them until 1949.

OPEN

ISLAMIC

ISLAMIC

GREEK

OFFICES

KITCHEN

PUBLIC
RESTAURANT

SARDIS
COLUMN

EXISTING SECTION LOOKING WEST

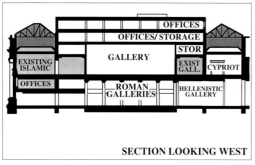

OFFICES

OFFICES/ STORAGE

STOR

GALLERY

EXIST
GALL.

CYPRIOT

EXISTING
ISLAMIC

OFFICES

ROMAN
GALLERIES

HELLENISTIC
GALLERY

SECTION LOOKING WEST

Gold bowl, Cypriot. 8th century B.C. The Cesnola Collection, Purchased by subscription, 1874–1876

the department, many of them distinguished collectors in this field who understand the enormous importance of this project; for in making the broad spectrum of the Greek and Roman holdings accessible to all visitors, the Metropolitan is giving long-overdue pride of place to the art that is the root of so much of Western civilization.

Although we have not yet worked out with any specificity the scheme of the installation, our thinking at the moment is to combine various media within each given culture—whether Minoan or Mycenaean, Attic or Etruscan—thus providing a more vivid, varied, and historical display. And in order to present a logical progression through the history of ancient Greece and Rome, we will reverse the current disposition of the collections and proceed in chronological sequence with Greek art shown first, off the Great Hall (see above) in the newly designated Robert A. and Renée E. Belfer Court (now devoted to Roman art). Greek art would also occupy the

reassessment of this department's collections, for the exacting and time-consuming work of conserving its vast number of pieces and formulating the concept that will govern the overall installation. Curator in Charge Carlos Picón has this responsibility, and he benefits from enthusiastic encouragement and support on the part of a group of friends of

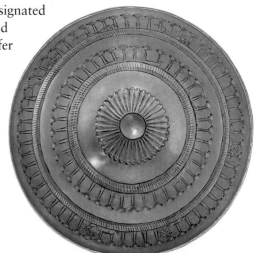

grand barrel-vaulted corridor (now used for Cypriot art and Roman frescoes) and the galleries on either side of it. Roman art would be exhibited in the skylit atrium that currently houses the public restaurant, in the adjacent service facilities that will be vacated, and on a newly built mezzanine level. The overall exhibition space will comprise 60,000 square feet. We will also fill in the attic above the atrium with a structure consisting of some 46,000 square feet for much-needed storage, offices, and perhaps some additional exhibition space.

In this scheme Cypriot works would be moved to the second floor contiguous to the Ancient Near Eastern collections, with which they have greater affinity than with classical art. At present only Cypriot sculpture is on view, but we will exhibit as well parts of our surprisingly rich holdings of terracottas and jewelry that have not been shown for decades.

In moving the restaurant and cafeteria, we will improve services to the public, by providing more seating capacity. Instead of one large eating facility with its inevitably long lines, there will be two separate new dining areas, one on the deck surrounding the Robert Lehman Wing and the other near the Costume Institute.

In perusing this publication, the reader will surely marvel at how much has been accomplished and at how many resources have been brought to bear on the projects that have literally doubled the square footage of both the public and service areas of the building. Perhaps most astonishing of all is that these efforts did not slow down our other activities; no educational program or public access was ever reduced. Quite the contrary. In fact, in the popular and highly visible arena of special exhibitions, the pace actually increased; and while we were building wing after wing and gallery after gallery, we were even devising ways to hoist on the façade not three but five banners to herald exhibitions.

Kevin Roche and Philippe de Montebello with a model of the Robert A. and Renée E. Belfer Court

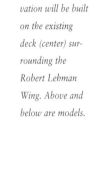

One of the new restaurants resulting from the Greek and Roman renovation will be built on the existing deck (center) surrounding the Robert Lehman Wing. Above and below are models.

such as "Canaletto" and "Seurat, 1859–1891." These are the rooms that should be used to display many of the paintings now confined to storage for lack of space, for future acquisitions, and perhaps even for whole collections—and history has kindly demonstrated that these may continue to come our way.

Three and even five banners attest to the increased pace of activity at the Met.

Indeed, a few years ago I pointed out to the Board of Trustees that what these splendid banners—this level of activity—conveyed was not so much "the glow of health as the flush of fever," and that I thought the institution could not indefinitely continue at such a pace in so many areas, particularly special exhibitions, without stretching its precious and finite resources of staff, time, space, and money. As it happens, the areas now devoted to special shows around the building will someday be reduced as we return—and we should—to the Department of European Paintings what we call the "B Galleries," the suite of rooms at the top of the Grand Staircase and just south of the Tiepolo gallery, where we have held exhibitions

This diminution of exhibition space may prompt or perhaps simply coincide with a concomitant slowing down of the exhibitions schedule; it may be achieved deliberately as a function of policy; or it may occur naturally as a consequence of the unfortunate conjunction of increased costs—especially in insurance and transportation—and reduced funding on the part of corporations and foundations, many of which have redirected their philanthropic dollars toward social and humanitarian causes. Here I would like to stress that I am not predicting the demise of large loan exhibitions, and only hesitatingly do I suggest that the overall pace will be reduced. I have eaten my share of hats over this issue, but the most memorably off-base pronouncement I can recall was Tom Hoving's in his preface to the catalogue of the tapestry exhibition in 1973, in which he states—and remember it was 1973!—that this exhibition would be one of the last of an era of large international loan shows, an era that was now coming to an end! As the large-exhibition era clearly has not come to an end—indeed, the activity has intensified in the intervening years—it is appropriate to discuss here, in talking about the future, just why this era is

likely to continue, albeit, perhaps, at a slightly slower pace or featuring more exhibitions smaller in scope and sharper in focus.

At the Metropolitan the collections remain the primary destination for most visitors, especially for those from out of town, who make up about 30 percent of our public; but for many people—particularly from the Tri-state area—the opening of a loan show is increasingly the reason for their visit. Because exhibitions are of a temporary nature, their novelty and newsworthiness make them the most visible and sought-after of the Museum's programs. The public obviously enjoys an attractive and well-informed exhibition, and the Museum benefits from increased attendance—we regularly and gladly cite the figures. But loan shows are expensive, funding is difficult, and the collections-related work of the institution is often disrupted. Why, then, when we have such extensive representative works of art in our own collections do we stage exhibitions? What is their precise value to the public and to the museum community?

Let me preface my response by noting that if the Metropolitan were to abandon exhibitions altogether and choose to operate simply as a repository for great works of art, handsomely and intelligently installed, it would remain a major resource and highest on the list of places to visit in New York. The Met is, in fact, now the number-one tourist attraction in the City, and most out-of-town visitors come regardless of what show is on view, so broad and fine are our collections of works from all parts of the world. School groups, of course, and tourists would continue to come in the same numbers, as they regularly do to the Cloisters, which does not mount exhibitions, but our large audience of repeat visitors would undoubtedly come less often, and they would feel a real sense of loss, as would the international community of scholars and connoisseurs.

This is not merely because exhibitions are glamorous activities, but because through them the Metropolitan Museum maintains its position worldwide as a potent force in inter-

Above: "Treasures of Tutankhamun," Dec. 1978–Apr. 1979. The figure is **Tutankhamun the Harpooner,** *lent by the Cairo Museum.*

Below: In "Degas," Oct. 1988–Jan. 1989, the Met's **Little Fourteen-Year- Old Dancer,** *H. O. Havemeyer Collection, Bequest of Mrs. H. O. Havemeyer, 1929*

with a large group of works by Rembrandt and Hals, but almost all are portraits. And although Dutch landscapes are well represented—except for marine painting—we are woefully deficient in the important genres of still life and biblical subjects. We boast five Vermeers, but we have no Saenredam. In truth, at the Metropolitan, as would be the case in any other general art museum, there is not a field in the history of art about which we

national exchanges and because they fulfill a critical, indispensable, art-historical, and educational function that is directly tied to the collections. Exhibitions are indispensable because the world's museums only in their aggregate can preserve mankind's artistic heritage. No single museum—not the Metropolitan, nor the Louvre, nor the Hermitage—can ever hope to represent any artist, style, or civilization so fully that exhibitions are not needed to complete the picture.

Museum collections, by their very nature and by the manner in which they were formed, reflect the specifics and limitations of the institution, the taste and wealth of a particular patron or donor, and those of the host region or city. Thus no matter how representative a museum's collection may be—and the Metropolitan's is about as rich and broad as can be found anywhere—it can never be truly, totally comprehensive. There is always some form of imbalance, both quantitative and qualitative. The Metropolitan, for example, is rich in Dutch seventeenth-century painting,

would not make a strengths-and-weaknesses assessment similar to that of our Dutch holdings. Exceptions are to be found, of course, in national museums, such as the Cairo Museum or the Archaeological Museum in Mexico City, that are devoted exclusively to the art of their own culture.

Loan exhibitions, then, are the means by which museums supplement the deficiencies in their own collections or build upon their own strengths. They can provide endless ways of exploring art in new and challenging juxtapositions, and since each work of art is unique, the presentation of those not ordinarily available is a source of both great joy and instruction.

Here I would like to mention our new policy of eliminating all ticketing systems and charges for special exhibitions, for although this issue is not related to the Master Plan, obviously, it does touch deeply on our mission to serve the public; and the elimination of ticketing illustrates clearly how serious the Museum is in its desire to make its collections and exhibitions truly accessible.

Ticketing, whether through advance sales or free on the same day, was cumbersome and restrictive. Advance sales called for booking a visit far ahead at a precise time—not the usual pattern for Museum visitors—and tended to deny entry to those who may have been unaware of the need for tickets, often out-of-towners, many of whom would not have had another chance to see the exhibition.

Ticketing of any sort had another, more serious drawback, that of discouraging the kind of viewing for which exhibitions are mounted in the first place. Most shows are rich in works that invite prolonged examination and call for levels of understanding that often require more than one visit. Also, visitors, delighted by these exhibitions, wanted to return, and some even several times. To discourage them was to betray one of the Museum's most cherished goals, to encourage random and repeat visits by the public.

Another factor that caused us to eliminate ticketing may seem paradoxical: namely, the occasional profitability of the venture. Simply put, the substantial revenue that could

Waiting in line for tickets to "Manet," held Sept. 10–Nov. 27, 1983

Right: "Al-Andalus: The Art of Islamic Spain," held in Spain at the Alhambra, in Granada (shown), Mar. 18–June 7, 1992, and at the Metropolitan, July 1– Sept. 27, 1992

Below: The international visitors' desk in the Great Hall

be realized from popular exhibitions caused wide swings in the budget from year to year, a phenomenon that was not healthy for the budgeting process nor for the integrity of the exhibitions program, which could not be allowed to suffer from pressure to mount more popular shows, shows planned not from any intellectual imperative but from the desire for more revenue. A bottom-line approach to exhibition programming, which would guarantee profits for some shows from advance ticket sales, would have had a rather insidious side, too, that of pitting one exhibition against another: it would give greater prestige to the ticketed exhibitions, presumed a priori to be perhaps more popular than the others on the schedule, but not necessarily more scholarly or important.

In doing away with ticketing, we were willing to accept possible short-term declines in revenue for the sake of sound museology.

I say "short-term," because in fact the elimination of ticketing represents not only a more civilized approach to accessibility, but it may also turn out to be, in the long run, financially rewarding as well. First of all, with repeat visits, attendance at exhibitions rises and along with it greater use of the Museum's revenue-producing activities, such as the restaurants, shops, and garage. Second, repeat visitors tend to become members; and, third, more visitors pleased with their experience and with their inevitable discovery of the permanent collections—which at the Metropolitan are along the routes to every show— mean an increase in our core group of regular, faithful visitors. That translates, year in and year out, into a higher attendance base and more predictable budgeting and, most important, into the fulfillment of our fundamental mission, namely, the introduction of more people to the wonder of art.

I have written in these pages of the importance of providing our visitors with the right ambience for the appreciation of art; our 1970 Master Plan had precisely this aim, of course, and so do our future projects, such as renovation of the Tiepolo gallery and of the Greek and Roman rooms. What I have not covered in any detail, and can only suggest here in the briefest way, are the myriad

improvements that still need to be made in a number of critical areas. Although this publication focuses mainly on new construction, we should not lose sight of the fact that most of our older structures date back more than a century and that in the next few years considerable resources will need to be devoted to their restoration and maintenance. There must be a substantial investment in modernizing our extensive and highly complex mechanical and electrical systems, such as security and climate control, if we are to reach the millennium with a sound, properly functioning building.

Other critical areas too briefly covered in these pages include services for the public. Of course, every square foot of the Master Plan was developed for the benefit of our visitors—after all, that is why we exist—but because this publication concentrates primarily on the collections and the building, other types of services specifically designed for the visitor have not been discussed. These include amenities such as more bathrooms and better directional signs, both of which, I am happy to say, will soon be addressed. More importantly, we will increase our efforts to make Museum visits even more congenial, as our newly instituted Friday and Saturday evening openings providing music, beverages, and walking tours have been extraordinarily well received.

Elsewhere, the growing demands on our resources by schools and other groups tell us that we should completely rethink the physical requirements of our education program. In 1981 a generous gift from Harold and Ruth Uris made possible the reorganization of spaces utilized by the education staff. Incorporating areas previously devoted to the Junior Museum, the resulting Ruth and Harold D. Uris Center for Education expanded our scope of public service, especially through the library and

resource room. Nevertheless, the present configuration of the Uris Center is now inadequate for our current needs.

As for our educational programs, they have grown and evolved along with the building expansion and the times, and they embrace a vast spectrum of tours, lectures, symposia and colloquia, concerts, talks, performances, workshops, and other activities of every description, all focused on the collections, our raison d'être. But no portfolio of

educational programs is ever permanently set, for concepts of study and teaching change with time, and our varied audience—or audiences—have different expectations and needs—from the schoolchild to the teacher; from the lay visitor to the art historian.

To cite one example, for a long while we lacked sufficient space for a quiet area for research and study in the Watson Library; and in 1980 we were able to remedy this situation with the addition, at the south end of the library, of the Jane Watson Irwin Center for Higher Education, which provides seminar rooms and more than fifty carrels for visiting scholars and staff.

Reading room in the exhibition "Seurat, 1859–1891," held at the Metropolitan, Sept. 24–Jan. 12, 1992, and jointly organized by the Réunion des Musées Nationaux, Musée d'Orsay, and the Metropolitan

A tour group in the Greek and Roman galleries

Right: Children in the Ruth and Harold D. Uris Center for Education using an interactive computer program, "Medieval Spain," produced by the Metropolitan

As audiences vary, so also do the means used by the Museum to communicate. Lectures and tours, handouts and catalogues, films and videos, and now the new electronic media that are changing our world are the tools through which we seek to animate the visual arts in our visitors' imaginations.

Indeed, the Metropolitan Museum has always prided itself on the use of available technology to serve its educational mission. We have been very active in publishing since our founding. We have also made films on art for most of this century and, more recently, videos. Now, with the arrival of the "information age," we will be participating in a technological revolution that will permit us to supplement dramatically the ways in which we communicate, both inside and outside the building. Among the major projects now under serious study is the capturing of underdeveloped attic spaces above the Great Hall and Grand Staircase to accommodate the Museum's extensive photographic archive and imaging operations and to provide for the creation of educational materials through conventional methods as well as through new communications technologies.

It is a too-little-known fact that The Metropolitan Museum of Art has the largest number of reproduction and documentary images of works of art in the Western Hemisphere (they number several million), and our opportunities to disseminate them widely will be all but limitless. We are now

studying the new technologies so as to harness them in the service of our educational mission, putting the Metropolitan Museum, quite literally, into every school and every home. That is the true meaning of the word "accessibility," not only to open our doors to those predisposed to cross our threshold but also to ensure that we encourage many more people to visit the Museum, to be introduced to the "wonder of art."

We need look no further, frankly, nor struggle with complex deontologies, nor engage in deep museological explorations to

know that the "wonder of art" is all at once the source and the aim of everything that we do. And if we do not lose sight of this and are ever mindful of maintaining, in every aspect of the Museum's operation, the tone and aura that are most conducive to each individual visitor's experience of art, then we can never go wrong. Fully confident of our role and place, we will know to manage our activities in just proportion, the watchwords of any judicious ordering of priorities.

Today we attract ever more visitors, and as our surveys show, more satisfied visitors than ever before. We should not view this with complacency, though, but remember that no matter how heartening are the present numbers, we should continue to further broaden our audiences—widening our outreach with the new media and imaging technologies, for example—so that it may truly be said that the Metropolitan belongs to all people. Broadening audiences, though, is not the same as merely increasing attendance, and we should always remember, when devising activities aimed primarily at increasing attendance, that first and foremost we must thoroughly understand and protect the quality of the experience our many visitors now seek—and find—at the Metropolitan. In this respect, I believe our real challenge in the future will not be how to find ways to transform ourselves, but rather how to maintain the quality of that experience in the face of whatever confronts us, whether budgetary crises or calls for radical change.

Every generation clamors for some form of change and brings its own orthodoxies to bear on its various demands. Swings in political thinking and shifts in fashion are the way of the world, and art museums, like other public institutions, must be alert and responsive to these changing needs of society. At the same time, we must bear in mind that such "swings" carry with them the notion of reversal, as in the action of a pendulum. Therefore the mix of what we do at the Metropolitan may vary and evolve according to the times, yet we remain true to the art—

inescapably of its own time and place—of which we are the trustees for posterity. For what our public derives from a visit to the Metropolitan, aside from "wonder" and aside from delight in contemplating some of man's greatest achievements, is the security and confidence that come from finding in the art on view a sense of permanence, of enduring quality—and a constant against which shifting fashions and ideas may be tested.

As we approach the new millennium, almost all of the projects referred to in this publication will have been completed. With the help of our friends and supporters, we will have built an institution that represents the culmination of policies born of clarity of purpose, of authority in the ordering of the collections, and of an ever-present sense of public-spiritedness. All of these, I believe, amply fulfill the trust placed in us by the Museum's founders when they created this wondrous institution in 1870 "for the purpose of...encouraging and developing the study of the fine arts,...of advancing the general knowledge of kindred subjects, and, to that end, of furnishing popular instruction and recreation."

In the European Paintings Galleries, a copyist working from The Harvesters, *by Pieter Bruegel the Elder, Flemish. Oil on canvas, dated 1565. Rogers Fund, 1919*

Photography

All photographs, unless otherwise noted,
by the staff of The Photograph Studio of The
Metropolitan Museum of Art. Photographers:
Joseph Coscia Jr., Katherine Dahab, Anna-Marie
Kellen, Oi-Cheong Lee, Patricia Mazza, Caitlin
McCaffrey, Bruce Schwarz, Eileen Travell, Karin
L. Willis, and Carmel Wilson

Marianne Barcellona, p. 45 (top); Bernstein
Associates, cover, pp. 23 (top), 81 (box, center);
Richard Cheek, p. 38 (bottom); Sheldan
Collins/Centaur Fine Arts Photography, p. 47
(top); Lynton Gardiner, p. 44 (dish); Fred George,
pp. 51 (top), 62; David Harvey, p. 86 (top); Sara
Krulwich–New York Times, p. 85; Derry Moore,
p. 55; Al Mozell, pp. 57 (top, left), 75 (top), 82, 83
(bottom), 84 (center, bottom); Newsday Photo, p. 10;
Cervan Robinson, p. 38 (top); Roche Dinkeloo
and Associates, pp. 16 (box), 21 (bottom), 64, 68
(top), 71 (models, bottom), 72 (box), 80 (box);
Brian Rose, pp. 16–17, 43, 54 (top); Brooks
Walker, pp. 4, 22 (bottom), 24, 34–35 (temple), 37
(top), 41 (top), 42 (top), 44 (bottom), 46 (bottom), 50, 53 (top), 73 (box), 86 (bottom); Bruce
White, p. 49 (top left, top right)

Plans, pp. 71 (center), 80 (top), by LaPlaca Design.
Designs, p. 74, by Stephen Saitas

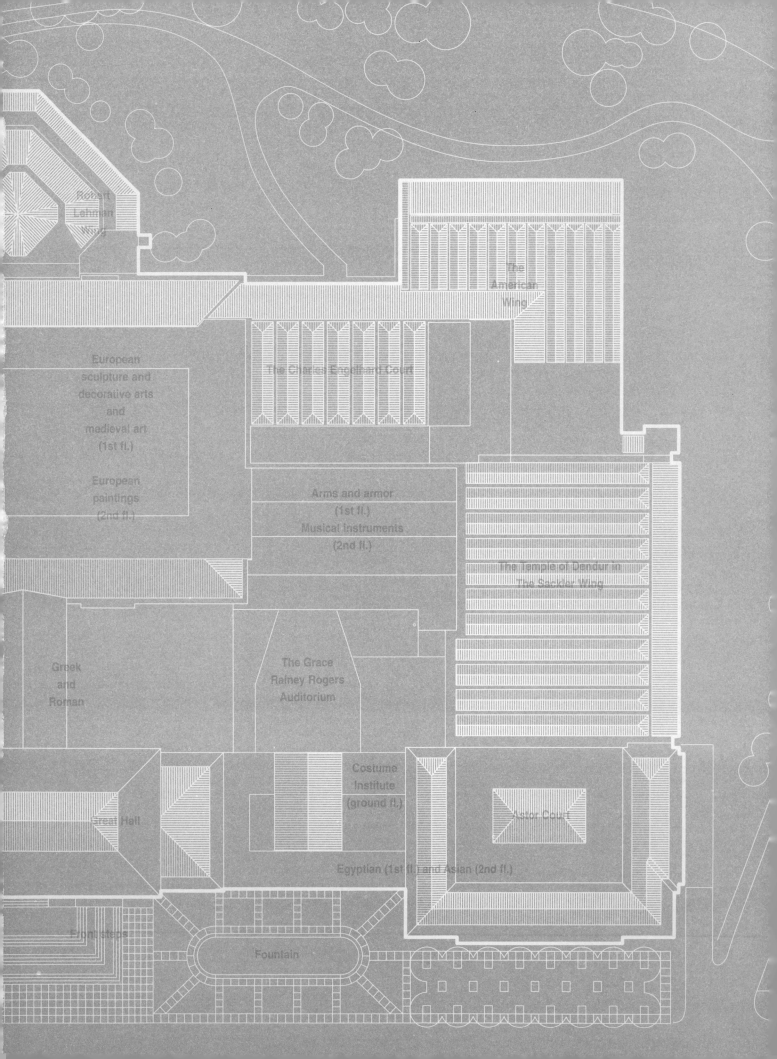

Robert
Lahman
Wing

The
American
Wing

European
sculpture and
decorative arts
and
medieval art
(1st fl.)

The Charles Engelhard Court

European
paintings
(2nd fl.)

Arms and armor
(1st fl.)
Musical instruments
(2nd fl.)

The Temple of Dendur in
The Sackler Wing

Greek
and
Roman

The Grace
Rainey Rogers
Auditorium

Costume
Institute
(ground fl.)

Astor Court

Great Hall

Egyptian (1st fl.) and Asian (2nd fl.)

Front steps

Fountain